HOMEGROWN
TEA

ALSO BY CASSIE LIVERSIDGE

Pasta Sauce! Grow Your Own Ingredients

HOMEGROWN TEA

An Illustrated Guide to Planting, Harvesting, and Blending Teas and Tisanes

CASSIE LIVERSIDGE

St. Martin's Griffin
New York

The author has researched each plant used in this book but is not responsible for any adverse effects any of the plants may have on an individual. One plant may be good for one person but have a negative effect on another. All the plants are consumed entirely at your own risk. Never use a plant as an alternative to seeking professional medical advice and always consume tea in moderation.

www.stmartins.com

The Library of Congress Cataloging-in-Publication Data is available upon request.

Book design by Michelle McMillian

ISBN 978-1-250-03941-5 (trade paperback)
ISBN 978-1-250-03942-2 (e-book)

St. Martin's Griffin books may be purchased for educational, business, or promotional use. For information on bulk purchases, please contact Macmillan Corporate and Premium Sales Department at 1-800-221-7945, extension 5442, or write specialmarkets@macmillan.com.

First Edition: March 2014

10   9   8   7   6   5   4   3

To

PETER,

GEORGE,

and

THOMAS

Contents

Introduction

Homegrown Tea is a gardening book for tea lovers. It explains how to grow a large variety of plants from which you can make teas and tisanes. Your own garden, balcony, or even windowsill could become your tea cupboard.

Teas and Tisanes

Tea has been grown in China for thousands of years, and all "tea"—white, green, oolong, or black—is made from one plant, *Camellia sinensis*. It is through methods of growing, harvesting, and processing that different-tasting teas are created. The Chinese held a monopoly on tea production for hundreds of years, but in the early ninth century, Buddhist monks travelled from Japan to China and brought back tea seeds, introducing tea growing to Japan. The Dutch were the first traders to import the drink to Europe and America. They traded through the port of Amoy in China, where the locals called this plant te, pronounced "tay." This was used and then translated into other languages as "tea" in English, or "Tee" in German. The Mandarin word *cha* was used throughout Persia, Russia, India, and Japan.

The expansion of commercial tea growing outside of China started in the 1840s with Robert Fortune, a British botanist. He went undercover as a tea merchant in China to gain vital knowledge of how to grow tea. He brought thousands of tea plants and skilled Chinese tea workers to British-ruled India. Tea is now grown commercially all over the world, including in the United States (South Carolina), Brazil, Ecuador, Turkey, The Azores, Argentina, and even England (Cornwall). Tea has been responsible for some major events in world history, including the Opium Wars in China and the Boston Tea Party, a key moment of the American Revolution.

Many other plants can be brewed just like tea leaves. Infusions of plants other than the tea plant should be called tisanes. For me, the word *tisane* does not conjure up the same sense of occasion and reverence as the word *tea* does, but I enjoy drinking tisanes as much as tea. I call all the infusions in this book teas to denote their importance as one of life's everyday pleasures, which I value greatly.

Top Tips to Brew the Best Cup of Tea

For all of the plants in this book, I give a recommended quantity for brewing one cup of tea. However, we all have different tastes, so feel free to increase or decrease the amount to suit your own. If you are making tea in a teapot for more than one person, increase the quantity of tea accordingly. You will need to use a tea strainer to catch the leaves when you pour the tea. The strained leaves can then be tipped back into the pot and used again. Homemade teas will often have a pale color, but the flavor can still be strong.

TEAPOTS

All high-quality teas have a certain teapot believed to be most suited to their flavor. The Yixing teapot is a tiny unglazed clay teapot that is said to enhance the flavor of oolong tea. Using a teapot is a wonderful way to share a tea but it must be used correctly or the flavor of the tea will spoil.

If you are using a teapot, you need to make sure that it contains the right amount of water for the number of cups you desire. The common mistake, because we have such big teapots, is to fill them to the top. The tea is poured for a first cup but then the tea leaves are left sitting in the remaining water for some time. The taste of the next cup will have deteriorated dramatically, and it can become very bitter. The best way to ensure the right amount of water goes into your teapot is to use the cup you will be drinking out of as a measure, according to

the number of cups of tea you are serving in one go (2 cup measure for 2 cups of tea). Pour the fresh boiled water (176° F/80° C) into your cup and then pour into the teapot containing the tea leaves. Then after a few minutes you can serve the tea, using a tea strainer and all of the water will be poured out of the teapot. The leaves will then sit in the teapot ready to be brewed again. You will get to know the correct quantity of water to use more intuitively after a while. Alternatively, buy a tiny teapot!

TEA BAGS

I have recommended brewing most of the teas in tea bags, as it is easier to give the cor-rect quantities of tea needed for one person and they are a great way to contain the plant so that you don't get bits in your tea. There are other tea infusers on the market you can use as an alternative or you can simply use the plant loose in a teapot. Tea bags have a bad reputation as they are often filled with poor quality tea and higher quality teas are always sold as loose-leaf. The key to mak-ing a wonderful cup of tea in a tea bag is giving the leaves room to move around and properly infuse the water. Using your own tea bags also allows you to reuse the bag to brew subsequent cups. The flavor of a sec-ond, third, and even fourth cup of tea is of-ten superior to the first cup, even if the same

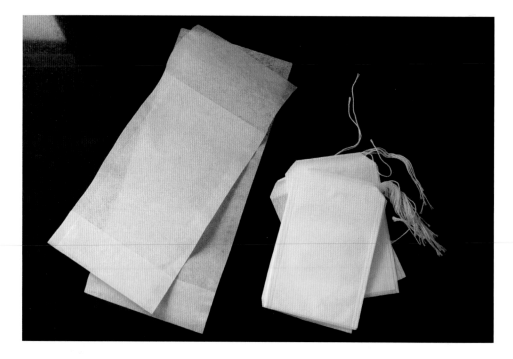

bag is used over a few days. All the plants have great capacity to keep exuding flavor.

Tea bags were first developed by accident in 1908 by Thomas Sullivan, a New York tea dealer. His wife made small silk bags as a means of sending samples of tea around the world. When the tea arrived, people thought the tea was supposed to be brewed in the bags, and the tea bag was born. Their popularity has grown ever since. Tea bags are filled by machine, and the tea needs to be very finely chopped in order to be able to be packed into these tiny bags. For the mass production of black tea for tea bags, a system of CTC—crush, tear, curl—is used. This speeds up the oxidation

process and creates tea that is small so it can easily be packed. This is a very harsh process that gives a strong rich taste, but the tea loses all subtlety and depth of flavor.

WATER

Another key to making the best tea is to always use fresh water to fill your kettle. It contains more oxygen, which will give a greater flavor to the tea. The temperature of the water is also important. You should never pour boiling water on your teas, as this destroys a lot of the flavor. Ideally, you want the water to be 176°F (80 to 85°C). To achieve this without needing to use a thermometer every time, boil the kettle using fresh water and wait for two minutes once it has been switched off before pouring the water onto your tea bag. I refer to this as "boiled water" throughout the book. You can use the water immediately after it has boiled to warm your teacup or teapot. Warming the vessels improves the flavor of the tea. Many tea connoisseurs wake up the tea leaves by giving them a rinse in the first-boiled (176°F/80°C) water and immediately pouring that water away. Then the leaves are wet and the first infusion is believed to taste better. Do employ this technique when you have time but I like to reuse the tea leaves and drink each cup to appreciate the variations in flavor.

If you are using the hard root or the rhizome of a plant instead of the leaves or seeds, you often need to make a decoction rather than an infusion. A decoction is a method of brewing your tisane in a pan, so that the root can be simmered for some time. The hard root then has time to soften. This allows the medicinal properties and flavor to come out of the root.

Medicinal Benefits of Tea

Tea was originally taken as a medicinal drink in China thousands of years ago. Other herbal plants have been taken as infusions for even longer. There is renewed interest in drinking tea for health reasons and in understanding more about the medicinal benefits of plants in general. Some of the plants in this book have "officinalis" in their names. This shows that the plant was recognized as "official" and "useful" and that it could be sold in an apothecary shop.

It is generally best to harvest plants first thing in the morning, before the sun and wind have had a chance to reduce the levels of medicinally beneficial oils.

I have given the medicinal benefits of each plant for general interest, but this should not be taken as medical advice. Always use herbs and plants with caution and consume in moderation. Always use the Latin name when buying a plant, as it is vital that plants are correctly identified. If you are unsure of a plant, do not consume it in any form.

Further Advice

There is a section at the back of the book with extra gardening and growing advice. Refer to it as needed. There is also advice on how to dry your plants for tea and how to make sun teas.

LEAVES

The Tea Plant

Camellia sinensis

There are hundreds of species of camellia plants, grown in gardens all over the world for their beautiful flowers and dark green glossy foliage. Only one species of camellia is used to make tea, however, and that is *Camellia sinensis*. All tea—white, green, oolong, and black—is made from this plant.

The tea plant is native to the high mountain ranges of the Yunnan province in southern China; *sinensis* actually means "from China." There are two main varieties from which tea is made, *Camellia sinensis* var. *sinensis* and *Camellia sinensis* var. *assamica*. *Camellia sinensis* var. *sinensis* (which I refer to as simply *sinensis* in this book) has smaller green leaves than assamica, and it is a strong hardy plant. This plant is best suited to the growing conditions in China and Japan. In 1823, Major Robert Bruce, who was working for the East India Company at the time, discovered *Camellia sinensis* var. *assamica* in Assam, in northern India. Assamica is grown predominantly in India, Africa, and Sri Lanka. Hundreds of hybrids and cultivars of these two varieties have been developed over the years.

Growing tea is as complex as growing grapes in a vineyard. The climate and soil directly influence the distinct flavor of the tea. Each country, each region, and even each producer will have their own distinct methods of growing and processing tea leaves. The world of tea is vast and the variations produced are many. Even tea produced on the same plantation over the course of one year can have large seasonal flavor differences. By growing your own tea, you will have the opportunity to experience your own homegrown tea flavor. In this chapter, I give a general and simplified introduction to the main differences between the methods of producing white, green, and black tea. I have created a way to process your own tea at home, based on information of how tea is processed

all over the world. You will be using tiny quantities of leaf and processing by hand, so the method and the results will be very different from tea grown and processed commercially. Even so, I hope it will give you an insight into the world of tea and help you to understand the tremendous experience and expertise tea producers have.

To Grow

Camellia sinensis loves to grow at high altitudes, where misty mornings and evenings allow the plant to absorb a lot of moisture. They like the warmth and light of the sun during the day. If you don't live at high altitude, do not fear—you can still grow

camellias. Try to plant your camellia in a sunny or partly shaded location and make sure that it has plenty of water—preferably rainwater—especially if you are growing it in a container.

It is very slow to grow tea from seeds. They take four to five weeks to germinate, so I recommend you buy one or two plants to start with. Tea plants are large enough to be harvested from when they are three or four years old, so try to get as mature a plant as possible. The *sinensis* variety is slower growing than assamica, and the leaves produce a lighter taste, but it is hardier and more resilient to frosts. Tea plants are not grown widely so you will probably not get a choice in which tea variety you can buy. I have listed a few suppliers in the back of this book.

You can grow your camellia in the ground or in a container. It needs well-drained, acidic soil with a pH of 5 or less. If your soil is not acidic, you can mix in leaf mold, bark, or mushroom compost. If your soil is very alkaline, it might be easier to grow camellias in a raised bed or a container. You may need to repot your camellia every one or two years, or when you first buy it if the roots are pot bound. Choose a container larger than the existing pot and make sure it has good drainage holes. Mix perlite (naturally occurring volcanic rock) or fine grit into ericaceous soil or acidic compost that is specially formulated compost for acid loving plants. (For more information about repotting, see page 255). They like a warm, sunny, or partly shaded location. They do not like direct heat over a prolonged time, such as next to a south-facing wall, so if you live in a warm climate, plant your camellia where it will have sun for part of the day and then shade. Mulch around your plant with bark to a depth of about 1 inch (2 to 3 cm). *Camellia sinensis* can tolerate cold and frost to 14°F (-10°C). If the plant is potted, however, the roots are more vulnerable to cold, especially if they are wet, so you may need to protect them with fleece. Fleece is a polypropylene fabric through which light, air, and rain can pass, unlike other fabrics. You can create a framework of canes around the plant and use pegs to attach the fleece, making sure the ground immediately around the plant is also covered. Or you can simply lay the fleece over the plant (and pot if its in one) so that it is totally covered, removing it if the temperature is warm enough during the day. It creates a warm pocket of air around the plant to help protect the leaves and roots from any drop in temperature. The more layers of fleece used, the greater the frost protection. Ask your supplier to give you specific advice on how many layers to use for your location.

On tea plantations, camellias are pruned to about 3 feet (1 meter) high so the new shoots grow at hand height. This is called the "plucking table," and you can do the same in your own garden if you have enough plants and space. This pruning promotes new shoots to grow. These fresh young leaves are referred to as the "flush." When the flush of growth appears in the spring, you will be able to harvest your tea. The length of the growing season depends on the amount of sunlight the plants receive. If the camellia's exposure to sunlight is shortened to less than eleven hours, it will become dormant and will not produce any new shoots until more daylight is available. This may mean that fewer new leaves are produced over the course of the year, but the quality of the tea produced after the plant has been dormant is excellent.

Camellia sinensis produces beautiful white, intensely fragrant flowers in the fall. For a wonderful variation of tea harvest these flowers and use them, fresh or dried, in addition to the leaves.

Feed the plants a nitrogen-rich feed, such as liquid seaweed, homemade nettle fertilizer, or worm tea, in the early spring and then again in May or June. (For more on fertilizer, see page 256). It will take about five years to grow a plant of a sufficient size to produce regular harvests. You can take cuttings of your camellias in the late summer.

To Take Cuttings

Cuttings should be taken from a developed leaf that is growing from a green stem.

1. Fill a pot with a mix of 50 percent horticultural silver sand and 50 percent ericaceous compost or acidic soil. Give the pot five taps on a flat surface to fill any air pockets within the soil. Make sure the pot is full of soil to the very top, adding more if necessary.

3. Cut the stem about ½ inch (1 cm) above the leaf, and about 1½ inches (4 cm) of stem below the leaf joint (node). Use a sharp knife and cut at an angle.

Using a toothpick, make a hole in the soil about ½ inch (1 cm) deep.

4. Hold the cutting at the node and insert it into the hole in the soil. Push down until your fingertips touch the soil. Make sure the leafstalk does not touch the soil.

5. The cutting should be planted so the leaf is almost vertical, so that over time it will not touch the soil, as this could cause it to rot.

Compact the soil tightly around the base of the cutting.

Lightly water the cutting.

6. Place a plastic bag over the top of the pot, supported on the outside by small canes or sticks—the bag should not touch the leaf. Secure it with a rubber band around the edge of the pot. Once you can see new growth developing you can remove the bag.

Keep the potted cutting somewhere warm and out of direct sunlight.

TIPS

Deer love to eat tea plants, so protect your plants with wire netting if you live in an area where deer are common.

WHITE TEA
Camellia sinensis

White tea, also called bud tea, is made with the soft, hairy tips of the *Camellia sinensis* plant. There is only one bud on each stem, and it must be harvested while it is still tightly twisted. The new buds are pale gray with silvery white hairs, hence the name "white tea." These precious thin buds are plucked carefully by hand to keep as many silver hairs attached as possible. The newest growth is the sweetest and subtlest tasting of all the teas. This may explain why white teas are so revered and can be so expensive.

Famous white teas include Yin Zhen or Silver Needles from Fujian Province, China. Regional variations in humidity, temperature, and soil conditions are some of the factors that contribute to the differing tastes of teas, so do not expect to achieve the level and depth of flavor of white tea as what is grown and produced by tea masters in ideal tea climates. You will be able to produce your own unique-tasting white tea, which will be mild, but sweet and delicious.

Medicinal Benefits

White tea is antibacterial and has high levels of antioxidants. It is also a stimulant, and it promotes a relaxed body and mind and can help with concentration. It is one of the most refreshing of all teas.

To Harvest

PLUCK

The pale gray, hairy leaf buds will only appear for a short time at the start of each growing season so be sure to keep an eye on your plants. Pluck the new leaf buds off while they are tightly bound.

WITHER

Spread the buds out on a tray or a fine mesh and leave them somewhere warm and well ventilated for a few hours to lightly wither them.

DRY

Place the buds in a dehydrator or a very low-temperature oven to remove the remaining moisture. Drying will not take long, so make sure you do not overdry the buds. The buds should be moved about throughout drying so that they dry evenly.

To avoid overdrying, I set my oven to 122°F (50°C), and when it is up to temperature I turn it off and then put the buds in to dry for about 20 minutes, moving them around every five minutes. (For more on drying, see page 259).

the warmed teapot. Pour the water (which should be between 176 to 185°F / 80 to 85°C) over the tea and cover it with a lid. Allow the tea to steep for three minutes. Remove the lid and the tea bag, or pour your tea from the teapot using a tea strainer. You should have a very pale yellow tea. This is a subtle, sweet, and delicious tea—one for a special occasion. Be sure to use the buds again for subsequent cups.

Tea Bag Friends

Don't share these precious tips with anyone!

TIPS

Yellow tea is in between white and green tea in terms of flavor and the amount of processing it receives. As with white tea, only the bud is used. After heating, the warm buds are covered with a cloth and allowed to slightly oxidize. Oxidation is a chemical reaction that occurs within the compounds in the leaf. The buds turn yellow, hence the name yellow tea. Such a refined process means these are very rare teas, so do try some at a specialist tea house if you have the opportunity.

To Make Tea

Fill the kettle with fresh water. Bring the water to a boil, then pour some into your teapot or teacup to warm it up. Discard the water. Put two or three pinches of buds (or more for a stronger flavor) into a tea bag or into

GREEN TEA
Camellia sinensis

Thousands of years ago in China, green tea was taken as a medicinal drink. It was the tea of choice in Britain until the middle of the eighteenth century, and it is still the most popular tea in China and Japan. It is enjoyed for its medicinal properties and for the stimulating effect it has on the body.

To make green tea, camellia leaves are heated before they can oxidize, so they retain their wonderful fresh green color and high levels of antioxidants. After this, there is a variety of ways to process the tea further. Buddhist monks developed a complex grinding process to make a powdered green tea known as matcha. In Japan there is a famous matcha tea ceremony, in which the powdered tea is whisked into a froth, poured, and consumed with great reverence.

Medicinal Benefits

Green tea is a stimulant and a diuretic, and is also antibacterial. It contains the highest levels of antioxidants of all the *Camellia sinensis* teas. It does contain a certain amount of caffeine, but the caffeine in tea is released slowly (unlike in coffee) so that it actually benefits the body and mind. Green tea also contains vitamins and iron and may help lower cholesterol and slow the aging process.

To Harvest

PLUCK

To make green tea, harvest the first burst of leaf growth from your *Camellia sinensis* plant. Your plants will put on new growth in the springtime when the weather warms, after the plant has been dormant over the winter. The new growth will have light

(1 cm) depth of water into the pan and set in the steamer insert. Cover with a lid and bring the water to a boil. When the water has come to a boil, remove the lid, drop the leaves into the steamer, and re-cover it. Steam the tea leaves for 1 to 2 minutes, until they start to turn an olive green color. Remove the pan from the heat and immediately run the leaves under a cold tap to stop the heating process and to retain as much green color as possible.

green stems, and the prior year's growth will have brown stems. Pluck the top two leaves and leaf bud from the tea plants.

HEAT

Heating the leaf will kill the enzymes within so that no oxidation can occur. This keeps the leaves greener. You can steam the leaves using a metal or bamboo steamer insert and a saucepan. Pour about ½ inch

ROLL

The leaves will be very soft and flexible and ready to be rolled. Rolling is the method of styling and shaping the leaf. To do this, simply roll the tea in your hands. Experiment with the shape you like. I like gently rolling the leaves in a sushi-rolling mat—you can get lovely even tubes this way. Place the leaves in the center of a bamboo sushi-rolling mat. Fold the mat in half over the leaves and, holding down the edge of the bottom half with one hand, push up on the top half of the mat with your other hand to roll the mat over the leaves. Roll the mat back and forth gently until the leaves are tightly rolled.

You can even try to roll your own green tea pearls! The highest quality gunpowder tea and jasmine pearl tea are still rolled by hand into tiny balls. If you have plucked the very freshest young new growth, roll-ing will only take 2 to 3 minutes, but if you have used older and harder leaves, it will take much longer.

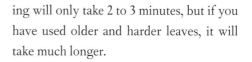

Immediately after rolling, spread the leaves out in a single layer on a baking dish or baking tray and place them in a preheated 212 to 230°F (100 to 110°C) oven for 10 to 12 minutes. After 5 minutes, give them a gentle turn to ensure uniform drying. When the leaves are totally dry and crispy,

they are done. The green tea is ready to be used immediately or can be stored in a sealed glass container in a dry, dark cupboard until needed.

How to Make Tea

It is good to keep the temperatures of all the vessels used to make the tea as constant as possible. Fill the kettle with fresh water. Bring the water to a boil, then pour some into your teapot or teacup to warm it up. Discard the water. Put six leaves of green tea into a tea bag or teapot—use more as necessary according to the number of people you are making tea for. Pour the water (which should be between 176 to 185°F/80 to 85°C) over the tea and cover it with a lid. Allow the tea to steep for three minutes. Remove the tea bag and set it on a saucer so that you can repeat the process for a second cup. Or pour your tea from your teapot, using a tea strainer. Enjoy the fresh sweet taste and the relaxing sensation of homegrown green tea.

TIPS

Made from partially oxidized leaves, oolong or wu-long tea has a taste between a green tea and a black tea. It combines the calming effects of green tea with the stronger flavor of black tea.

Tea Bag Friends

- Green tea is well suited to the fragrance of flowers. You can add dried flowers such as camellia, rose, and violet to your jars of dried green tea leaves to create your own flower-scented green tea. Jasmine tea is essentially green tea flavored with the scent of the jasmine flowers. See Jasmine, page 191, for more instructions.

- Commercially available "flowering teas" are created using dried flowers that are rolled within green tea leaves. It takes a great deal of skill to create flowering teas. They can be large balls, depending on the flower used, and are an amazing tea to watch infuse. You should drink these in a glass or infuse them in a glass teapot so that you can see the spectacle of it.

BLACK TEA
Camellia sinensis

Black tea is made from completely oxidized leaves of the *Camellia sinensis* plant. The tea is a dark color and has a strong rich flavor. *Camellia sinensis* var. *assamica* is the variety of camellia preferred for the production of black tea. Its leaves are bigger than those of *Camelia sinensis* var. *sinensis* and have greater surface area, allowing more oxidation to take place. It is the oxidation or fermentation that makes the leaves turn dark brown or black, as the name suggests.

Medicinal Benefits

Antioxidants found in black tea are believed to help prevent heart disease, some cancers, and strokes. It may also help with circulation and reduce fatigue. Black tea is a diuretic so it helps to detoxify the body.

To Harvest

When tea is grown at a high altitude in countries like India, plucking of tea traditionally takes place early in the morning,

before the sun has a chance to heat and dry the morning mist covering the leaves.

PLUCK

Pluck the top two leaves and bud to make into black tea. Make sure you only pick a few leaves at a time if your plants are small. The leaves make the plant's food, so if you take too many in one go, the plant will struggle to survive.

WITHER

Spread the leaves on a mesh screen or a tray and set them inside or outside on a cool, dry day. Allow them to wilt for up to twenty hours after which the leaves will have lost about 60 percent of their moisture. You can weigh the leaves to be exact, but as long as the leaves look and feel limp this is fine.

ROLL

You can roll the leaves between the palms of your hands. This rolling ruptures the cells of the leaves, so that all the juices and natural chemicals combine with each other. This reaction turns the leaf brown, and is called oxidation or fermentation. I like using a sushi-rolling mat to roll the tea on, as you can get lovely tubes of tea. Place the leaves in the center of a bamboo sushi-rolling mat. Fold the mat in half over the leaves and, holding down the edge of the bottom half with one hand, push up on the top half of the mat with your other hand to roll the mat over the leaves. Roll the mat back and forth gently until the leaves are tightly rolled.

OXIDIZE

Immediately after rolling, spread the leaves out in a single layer on a tray or baking

dish. Leave them to oxidize at room temperature, ideally between 69 to 75°F (21 to 24°C), for up to three hours. The leaves will turn brown as they oxidize.

DRY

Place the leaves in a preheated 230 to 257°F (110 to 125°C) oven to dry for about 20 minutes. When the leaves are crispy, they are completely dry and ready to be used. Once cooled to room temperature, store the leaves in a sealed glass container in a cool dark cupboard until needed.

To Make Tea

Homegrown black tea is much weaker than professionally processed black tea. Fill the kettle with fresh water. Bring the water to a boil, then pour some into your teapot or teacup to warm it up. Discard the water. Put three or more pinches of tea into a tea bag or teapot. Pour the water (which should be between 176 to 185°F/80 to 85°C) over the tea; if using a teapot, pour the water into the teapot and cover it with a lid. Allow the tea to steep for three to four minutes. Remove the tea bag or pour the tea from the teapot using a tea strainer. Serve without milk and sugar. Homegrown black tea is a pale brown color and has a delicious, refreshing, sweet taste.

Tea Bag Friends

- Black tea is lovely served with a slice of fresh or dried lemon.

- Black tea blends well with many other teas. You can make up bags or jars of black tea with lavender flowers, violets or strawberries in advance, so that the flavors can blend together over time.

TIPS

There are many types of black teas available to buy. Lapsang suchong is made from black tea leaves that have been smoked and infused with the scent of pine needles. Earl Grey tea is black tea leaves infused with essential oil from the skin of the bergamot (*Citrus bergamia*) fruit.

Anise Hyssop
Agastache foeniculum

Anise hyssop is from the Lamiaceae (mint) family and is native to the western United States. It has light green, heart-shaped leaves with serrated edges, tinged with purple in the spring. The leaves give out a wonderful aniseed smell when they are rubbed. Bees and insects love anise hyssop flowers because they are rich in nectar, so it is a great plant to help attract wildlife to your garden. It is sometimes referred to as hummingbird mint. Both the flowers and the leaves can be used to make a delicious fragrant tea. Do not confuse it with hyssop (*Hyssopus officinalis*), star anise (*Illicium verum*), or aniseed (*Pimpinella anisum*), which are different plants.

Medicinal Benefits

Native Americans have used anise hyssop as a medicinal plant for hundreds of years. They use it as a remedy for coughs and to help fight colds and fevers.

It is also believed to help with rheumatic pain. If you are pregnant, research possible side effects of this herb before using.

To Grow

Buy a plant instead of starting from seed, so that you can harvest anise hyssop tea in the first year. Anise hyssop likes well-drained soil and plenty of sun. It grows to about 2 to 3 feet tall (90 cm) by about 1 foot (30 cm) across, so plant it at the back or middle of a border to allow for its height. It will flower from summer through autumn and will give your garden lovely color for many months. Like other members of the mint family, it can spread easily. If not kept under control, it can take over a small garden; you can keep it in a planter or tub if you do not want this to happen. Fill a planter with a mixture of potting soil and grit or sharp sand to help improve drainage, and keep it well watered. Feed the plant with an organic fertilizer early in the spring if it is in a container. It will not survive very cold frosts or temperatures below 21°F (-6°C), especially if it is growing in a pot. During cold weather, bring it into an unheated greenhouse or protect it with horticultural fleece.

Anise hyssop is an herbaceous perennial plant so it will die back every winter and appear again in the spring. Should you need more plants, you can take cuttings in the spring or dig the plant up and divide the roots (see page 255). At the same time, prune back the whole plant to encourage fresh, healthy new growth for the forthcoming year. You can collect the seeds in the late autumn for future sowing or to give to friends.

To Harvest

The plant can be harvested anytime from May until it dies back in late fall. If you want to harvest its flowers, too, these will continue from June/July through September and possibly October. Pick leaves and flowers as and when you need them for a cup of fresh anise hyssop tea.

To dry the plant to store and use throughout the year, pick as many leaves and flowers as you think you may need, but making sure that enough are left on the plant so that it will continue to grow. It is preferable to pick in the morning on a dry, sunny day. Cut the stems about 4 inches (10 cm) from the base of the plant. Group your harvest into small bunches. Tie the stems of each bunch together with an elastic band and hang them upside down in a dry, well-ventilated place. When the leaves and flower heads are totally dry, break them off of the stems; break up the leaves to make them smaller. Alternatively chop the young stems up into ½ inch (1 cm) long pieces with the leaves attached, or remove the leaves from older stems, and dry flat on a tray or in a dehydrator. Store the dried leaves and flowers in a sealed glass container somewhere dark and dry until ready to use.

To Make Tea

Fill the kettle with fresh water. Bring the water to a boil, then pour some into your teacup or teapot to warm it up. Discard the water. For a cup of fresh anise hyssop tea, remove two or three leaves and a flower, tear them into smaller pieces, and put them into a tea bag or teapot. If using dried anise hyssop, use one pinch of dried leaves and flowers. Pour the boiled water (which should be between 176 to 185°F/80 to 85°C) over the tea. Cover with the saucer or lid to contain the aroma. Allow the tea to steep for three to five minutes. Remove the tea bag or pour the teapot using a tea strainer, putting a fresh leaf in the teacup to serve. The tea has a delicious mild anise flavor.

TIPS

The fresh leaves are wonderful mixed into a salad or put into stir-fries. When using the leaves in cooking I recommend chopping them up, as they can be a little tough to chew. Anise hyssop flowers retain color and scent when dried, so they are great to use in potpourri.

Tea Bag Friends

• Try blending anise hyssop with a decoction of rose hips (see Rose Hip, page 162). Strain the rose hip decoction into a teacup containing a tea bag of anise hyssop. Infuse for three minutes, then remove the tea bag and enjoy. This tea is very good to help with coughs and colds.

• Try blending anise hyssop with honeysuckle for a soothing and warming tea. Put a pinch each of anise hyssop and honeysuckle in a tea bag or teapot, and steep in boiled water for three minutes. Remove the tea bag or pour the tea from the teapot using a tea strainer.

Bergamot

Monarda

This plant genus was named *Monarda* after Dr. Nicholas Monardes, a Spanish botanist and physician who first documented it in 1571. Bergamot (*Monarda*) is also called bee balm, red bergamot, or Oswego tea. Around the time of the Boston Tea Party, early settlers needed to find a substitute drink in place of heavily taxed, imported tea. They saw Monarda being made into tea by the Oswego Indians in New York State (hence the name Oswego Tea). It gained its most common name, bergamot, from its flavor, which is similar to that of the bergamot orange plant (*Citrus bergamia*). Bergamot orange is used to flavor Earl Grey tea. The plants are not related.

There are many species of *Monarda* and even more cultivated varieties of the plant. I suggest finding one that is suited to growing in your location and that has the most fragrant leaves and flowers. *Monarda didyma* (red bee balm) has flowers composed of bright red tubular petals in the summer and fragrant leaves. *Monarda fistulosa* is a wild bergamot native to the United States and Canada. The pale mauve flowers provide an important food source for bees and other pollinating insects. *Monarda punctata* has pale pink flowers and is believed to contain the greatest medicinal strength of all the *Monardas*. It is native to Florida, where it is also called horsemint or spotted bee balm. There is also lemon bergamot (*Monarda citriodra*), sometimes called lemon mint, an annual plant with beautiful pink flowers and lovely lemon-flavored leaves. The leaves and flowers from all of the many different species and cultivars of *Monarda* can be used to make wonderful teas.

Medicinal Benefits

Bergamot is high in antioxidants, vitamin A, and vitamin C. It is an antiseptic so it may be good for sore throats and colds. It is a very calming plant and has been used to treat depression. Native Americans used the plant to treat nosebleeds, insomnia, fevers, and stomachache.

To Grow

Bergamot is easy to grow from seed in the early spring. (For more on growing from seed, see page 253.) Bergamots belong to the Lamaiceae, or mint, family, so bear this in mind when choosing where and how to grow it as it can take over a small plot. If you have lots of space, it can be beautiful in an herbaceous border, but remember to plant it toward the middle or back of the bed as it can reach 3 feet (90 cm) tall. Bergamot needs good ventilation, so allow 2 feet (.60 cm) between your plants. Bergamots like moist, well-drained soil, and they are not fussy about the soil type (pH level). They ideally like to be planted in a partly shaded area, but they can grow in full sun if you use mulch to help retain moisture to keep the roots cool. You can grow bergamot in a container as long as it is deep enough (at least 1 foot/30 cm) to give the roots room to grow and so it does not too easily dry out. They are susceptible to mildew, a white

powdery fungal infection of the leaves, due to lack of water. If this is a reoccurring problem, try spraying the leaves with milk when the disease is first detected and water well. Otherwise, mildew-resistant varieties are available. Divide your plants every three years, every two if they are growing in a container. Fertilize the plants in the springtime to encourage healthy new growth. They can get green flies around the tender new buds, so keep an eye out for flies and squash them when you see them, or use a garlic spray before they have a chance to take over. Bergamot is hardy so does not require winter protection. It will die back during the winter months and re-sprout again the following spring.

To Harvest

As with most plants, the leaves have the best flavor and medicinal value before the flowers appear. You can harvest some of these smaller leaves earlier in the summer before the tall flower stems grow. Allow some stems to grow on so they can produce flowers that can also be used in your bergamot tea. Cut the stems to just above a leaf joint as this will encourage the plant to bush out.

Pick the leaves off the stems and cut up the smaller stems to use as well. On the larger flowering stems, tear the leaves into smaller pieces. Do not use the large thicker stems as they are too hard. To bergamot, separate the torn flowers and small stems from the leaves and dry them separately, as the leaves will take less time to dry. Use a dehydrator, or lay the bergamot on a tray or mesh and leave somewhere warm and well ventilated, to gently dry (see page 260). Turn the leaves frequently to aid the drying process. Once completely dry and crispy, store in a sealed glass container somewhere dark and dry until needed.

To Make Tea

Fill the kettle with fresh water. Bring the water to a boil, then pour some into your

for three minutes. Lift the tea bag up and down a few times to aid the infusion, then remove it. If using a teapot pour the tea using a tea strainer. You can add a small flower to the teacup for a very decorative tea. The stems and the flowers have the same sweet, slightly spicy, lemony scent and it has a rosemary flavor with a hint of mint and oregano. It is a warming and relaxing tea.

Tea Bag Friends

- Blend bergamot with black tea to make your own version of Earl Grey. Combine black tea and dried bergamot in a container, seal it, and allow the flavors to blend together over a few days.

- Blend bergamot with rosemary for a "feel-good" tea. Put a small pinch of both plants into a tea bag or teapot and add boiled water. Steep for 3 minutes. Remove the tea bag or pour from the teapot using a tea strainer.

TIPS

Bergamot can be used in place of oregano in lots of culinary dishes, including pasta dishes.

teacup or teapot to warm it up. Discard the water. You can use bergamot fresh from the plant or dried. Put five or so small fresh or dried leaves and a pinch of broken flower into a tea bag or teapot. Pour the boiled water (which should be between 176 to 185°F/80 to 85°C) over the tea. Cover with a lid. Allow the tea to steep

Cardamom

Elettaria cardamomum

Green cardamom, or true cardamom, grows wild in the forests of India and Sri Lanka. Although the plant is known primarily for its seeds, it has aromatic leaves that can be used in cooking as well as for making tea. The leaves are dark green, with a lighter green underside and long stems. New leaves are bright green and much thinner and more delicate. They have a wonderful spicy, aromatic smell and taste similar to but distinct from the seeds. There is written evidence that cardamom has been used as a medicinal plant as far back as the second century BC. It has been in cultivation in Asia for hundreds of years and has been grown in the shade of *Camellia sinensis* on large tea plantations in India. Cardamom belongs to the Zingiberaceae, or ginger, family, and its seeds are one of the most highly prized of all spices. Green cardamom powder is used in Kashmir and other central Asian countries as a flavor in a tea called *khawa*. It is also used in Asia as an ingredient in masala chai, a spiced tea that also contains ginger, cinnamon, cloves, and pepper. Black cardamom (*Amomum subulatum*) is from a different genus in the same family and has larger, dark brown seeds.

Medicinal Benefits

Cardamom is anti-inflammatory and is believed to help with sore throats and colds. It is used to aid digestion and calm upset stomachs, and may be helpful in treating stress and depression.

To Grow

It is very difficult to grow cardamom from seed. The seeds must be sown in a specific and limited time after they have ripened; the seeds you buy at the grocery store for cooking were picked before they ripened, so they will never germinate.

You will need to buy a cardamom plant to start off with. It needs to be grown inside unless you live in a tropical climate, as it likes to be kept at 71°F (22°C) or above all year. Cardamom loves a humid environment, so a bathroom windowsill is perfect for the plant. They don't like to be in a very sunny position. Once you have found the perfect spot for this attractive houseplant, do not move it around, as it does not like change. The plant should stay neat and compact when grown inside, unlike when it is grown in the wild, when it can grow 22 feet (6 to 7 meters) tall. Restricting its size will mean that your cardamom is very unlikely to make fruit and seed.

To make more plants, you can divide your plant in the spring. Like ginger, cardamom has rhizomes (underground swollen stems) that can be divided using a knife. Feed your cardamom an organic houseplant feed or liquid seaweed in the spring. Remove any dead leaves by pulling or cutting them off at the base of the stem. Cardamom plants can become quite congested with dead stems and leaves, so make sure you cut them back to the base of the plant. If the tips of the leaves turn brown, the plant is being overwatered.

To Harvest

Harvest only the young light green leaves or any leaves that have grown since you have been caring for the plant. This is to ensure that you will not be using any leaves that may have been sprayed with any chemicals before you bought the plant. Cut off the leaves at the base as needed, as it grows new leaves all the time when grown indoors. Chop up the leaves and the stalks. You can use cardamom fresh or dry it for later use. Dry the cardamom leaves in a dehydrator, or spread the leaves out on a baking tray and put into a low temperature oven 212° F (100° C), or somewhere warm and well ventilated, turning the leaves every so often. They will give off an amazing aroma when touched. When completely dry and crispy, store in a sealed glass container somewhere dark and dry until needed.

To Make Tea

Fill the kettle with fresh water. Bring the water to a boil, then pour some into your teacup or teapot to warm it up. Discard the water. Put a large pinch of dried cardamom into a tea bag or teapot. Pour the boiled water (which should be between 176 to 185°F/80 to 85°C) over the tea and cover with a saucer or a lid. Allow the tea to steep for three minutes. Remove the tea bag or pour the tea from the teapot using a tea strainer. Drink and enjoy. The tea has a lovely sweet pungent flavor and is wonderfully warming on a cold night.

TIPS

The leaves can also be used for cooking, and are great wrapped around fish or chicken. Cardamom seeds are sometimes chewed and used as a breath freshener after a meal.

Tea Bag Friends

• Cardamom is wonderful blended with saffron, as the saffron gives this otherwise clear tea a yellow color. Put a small pinch of cardamom and a large pinch of saffron into a tea bag or teapot and add boiled water. Steep as before. This is a great pick-me-up tea to help lift your mood and to help with stress.

• Cardamom is also lovely blended with fresh or dried ginger. Put a small pinch of each in a tea bag or teapot and enjoy.

Hyssop

Hyssopus officinalis

This is a beautiful herb that is surprisingly little known or used today. Hyssop is an evergreen perennial originally from the Mediterranean. European colonists introduced this medicinal plant to North America where it can now be found growing wild in some states. Blue hyssop is the wild variety, but you can also find white hyssop (*Hyssopus officinalis ("Alba")*) and pink hyssop (*Hyssopus officinalis "Roseus"*). All three are suitable to use for making tea.

Hyssop has small, thin, pointed, dark green leaves that have a lovely rich aromatic scent when rubbed. It has clusters of small, trumpet-shaped flowers along the stems, and it flowers all the way through the summer. Bees and other pollinating insects love it. The leaves, green stems, and flowers are used to make hyssop tea.

Medicinal Benefits

Hyssop is an antiseptic, and is believed to help with sore throats, colds, and coughs, as well as bronchitis and asthma. It may also help increase your energy levels. Do not use hyssop if you are pregnant.

To Grow

You can grow blue hyssop from seeds easily in the spring (see page 253). If you are in a rush to try the tea, you can buy a small plant to start off with. In the summer you can repot your hyssop into a larger container or plant it in your garden in a sunny area. Mix in one handful of perlite or grit for every handful of potting soil, as hyssop loves very free-draining soil. It will not need much watering and can be kept on the dry side. Hyssop is a lovely plant to have in a pot next to your door so you can smell it when you brush past. You can propagate cuttings in the spring once the plant is established, especially from pink or white varieties as these may revert to another color if grown from seed.

Blue hyssop is fully hardy but the white and pink cultivars are less tolerant of frosts and temperatures below 23°F (-5°C), so they may need to be protected with a fleece. If the hyssop is growing in a container, it will benefit from a feed of seaweed or another organic fertilizer in the summer. It may die back slightly in the winter and need pruning in spring to promote new growth. Its older stems become woody over time so pruning will keep the plants fresh and neat.

To Harvest

You can harvest hyssop anytime during the growing season from spring though summer. Use scissors to cut off some green stems. If harvesting in summer, you will be able to harvest both the flowers and the leaves. Chop up the stems into small pieces about ½ inch (1 cm) long. Thicker stems will be too hard to cut, so peel the leaves off of these and discard the thick stem. Hyssop can be used fresh or dried for later use (see page 182). To dry, lay the flowers, leaves, and chopped stems on a baking sheet or dish and set them in a low temperature oven, dehydrator, or airing cupboard. You can also dry small bunches by tying them with a rubber band and hanging them upside down in a dry, dark room. Once totally dry and crispy, store in a sealed glass container somewhere dry and dark until needed.

To Make Tea

Fill the kettle with fresh water. Bring the water to a boil, then pour some into your teacup or teapot to warm it up. Discard the water. Put two pinches of fresh or dried hyssop into a tea bag or teapot. Pour the boiled water (which should be between 176 to 185°F/80 to 85°C) over the tea and cover with a saucer or lid. Allow the tea to steep for three minutes. Remove the tea

Tea Bag Friends

- Blend with strawberries or blueberries for an antioxidant-boosting tea. Put two or three slices of strawberry or two pinches of ground blueberry and a small pinch of hyssop leaves into a tea bag or teapot and pour over boiled water. Steep for three to four minutes. Remove the tea bag or pour the tea from the teapot using a tea strainer.

- For a tea to help coughs and sore throats, infuse a tea bag of hyssop into a decoction of echinacea (see Echinacea, page 234). Strain the Echinacea decoction into a teacup containing a tea bag of hyssop. Infuse the tea bag for three minutes and then remove to drink.

TIPS

Hyssop can be used in stews, stuffings, and soups and sparingly in salads. Do not confuse this plant with anise hyssop (see page 21) or water hyssop. They are completely different plants.

Warning: Not to be used by pregnant women.

bag or pour the tea from the teapot using a tea strainer. The tea is a pale blue-green color and has a fresh, green, rosemary-like aroma. It has a gentle taste of rosemary with a hint of lemony mint flavor. A very sweet and soothing tea.

Lemon Balm
Melissa officinalis

emon balm has been used by many cultures as a medicinal herb for thousands of years. It is native to southern Europe and western Asia. The *officinalis* in its name actually means "used in medicine." It is a perennial herb and will die back in the winter and reappear the following spring. From June to October, it produces small, whitish flowers that are a good source of nectar and pollen for bees. They are also edible. Lemon balm has slightly rough, scoop-edged, hairy leaves that are a medium green color and smell strongly of lemon when rubbed.

Medicinal Benefits

Lemon balm has been used to help with indigestion, including the feeling of bloating. It is believed to help the memory, lift spirits, and help combat depression. It is also antiviral and antibacterial, and contains vitamin C.

To Grow

You can grow lemon balm easily from seed. Start your seeds inside in the early spring and sow them according to the instructions on the packet (see page 253 for more on sowing). Sow in a mixture of equal parts perlite and potting soil for good drainage. Do not overwater.

If you start with a small plant, you should be able to use its leaves for tea in its first year. It can be planted in your garden in a sunny or partly shaded spot. It can easily be grown in a pot or container, as it is invasive in a garden (it is in the mint family). If growing lemon balm in a container, feed the plant in the springtime with an organic fertilizer such as liquid seaweed or worm tea. You should repot the plant into a larger container each year to give it more room to grow (see page 255). Once it is established you can divide the plant by pulling apart the roots and repotting. Cut back woody stems in the early spring to tidy up the plant and promote new growth.

Lemon balm can get whitefly under its leaves, so if you notice any insects, squash them with your fingers and keep a close eye out for any others. You can also spray the underside of the leaves with a garlic spray on consecutive days. Make sure the plant has good ventilation to help prevent diseases and pests.

To Harvest

Pinch off the leaves when needed; the freshest youngest growth is always recommended. Leaves and flowers can be used fresh, or dried for use throughout the year. Harvest a larger amount in the late summer before the plants go to seed. To dry, pick the leaves off the stem. Spread them out in a single layer on a baking sheet or mesh screen. I find that drying in the oven is too harsh for these leaves. They keep a brighter green color if they are gently dried in the warm air near a radiator or in a warm room and turned every so often. When completely dry and crispy, store in a sealed glass container in a dry, dark cupboard.

To Make Tea

Fill the kettle with fresh water. Bring the water to a boil, then pour some into your teacup or teapot to warm it up. Discard the water. Put two pinches (about five leaves) of either fresh or dried lemon balm into a

tea bag or teapot. Dried lemon balm may have a stronger taste than fresh. Pour the boiled water (which should be between 176 to 185°F/80 to 85°C) over the tea. Cover with a lid and allow the tea to steep for three minutes. Remove the tea bag or pour the tea from the teapot using a tea strainer. The tea has a delicious lemon flavor and a relaxing effect. Enjoy.

TIPS

You can use lemon balm in pot-pourri. Also, if you rub the leaves on your skin, it will act as a natural insect repellent. Some people's skin may react to this, so test a small area first and use with caution.

Warning: As with all herbs, do not take lemon balm in place of consulting a doctor or medical practitioner. Lemon balm should not be used if you are on a sedative or thyroid medication.

Tea Bag Friends

- To help induce relaxation and sleep, mix a small pinch of lemon balm with a small pinch of chamomile into a tea bag or teapot and pour on boiled water. Steep for three minutes. Remove the tea bag or pour from the teapot using a tea strainer.

- For a memory boosting tea, blend lemon balm with a pinch of pineapple or tangerine sage. Put a pinch of each into a tea bag or teapot and brew as above.

- You can also drink lemon balm as an iced tea, blended with stevia and lavender. Put a pinch of each into a tea bag or teapot and pour on boiled water. Infuse for three minutes. Remove the tea bag or pour the tea from the teapot using a tea strainer. Allow the tea to cool and then place in a refrigerator. When chilled served with lavender flowers frozen in ice cubes or a fresh lavender flower.

Lemongrass

Cymbopogon citratus

Lemongrass is native to Asia where it has been used as a medicinal herb for centuries. It has long, slender green leaves on hard purple-tinged stems called culms. The leaves have a beautiful lemon scent when brushed. It is a tender perennial so it may need to be brought inside during the winter, depending on your location. If grown in a tropical climate, it is an evergreen plant and can grow up to 6 feet (2 meters) tall. There are fifty-five species of *Cymbopogon*, including *Cymbopogon nardus*, commonly referred to as citronella grass, from which citronella oil is made. You can use the culm or stem of *Cymbopogon citratus* to make tea, but I want to show how the leaves can also be utilized, as they are delicious and often overlooked.

Medicinal Benefits

There are believed to be many health benefits to drinking lemongrass tea. The leaves are high in folic acid, vitamin C, and vitamin B. Lemongrass is known to help improve digestion and calm nervous stomachs. It is also an antiseptic, and helps fight coughs and colds. It is a natural diuretic so it will help flush toxins from your body and keep you healthy.

To Grow

It can take time and patience to germinate lemongrass from seed. Sow early in the year. The seeds only need a very thin layer of soil to cover them. To help speed up germination, place a plastic bag over the container to help create a warm, moist environment. If they dry out, the seedlings are quick to die. (For more information on sowing, see page 253.)

In order to have some leaves to harvest in the first year, I recommend buying a plant to start off. It can be grown in your garden but it will not withstand temperatures less than 48°F (8°C), so you will need to bring it in during the colder months. It can happily grow inside as a houseplant in a sunny conservatory or greenhouse, where there is light and warmth. In the late

fall, the leaves will start to turn brown because of the lower light levels. As soon as you notice this, use scissors or secateurs to cut back the whole plant to a height of 8 to 9 inches (20 cm), and harvest the leaves for your tea. The plant will then become dormant over the colder months. It requires

very little water at this time. If you live in a climate that does not experience frosts, your lemongrass may survive outside all year round.

The following spring, when the weather warms, new shoots will start to grow. Lemongrass needs full sun and a sheltered position. Feed your lemongrass with a good organic fertilizer throughout the summer. Remove any dead leaves from the plant by pulling them from the culm so the whole leaf is removed. When your plant is really established you can divide it to make more plants (see page 251).

You can also grow new plants from the stems you buy at grocers. Buy three stems which still have their base on (sometimes they are cut off too high), remove a couple of leaves, and place the stem in a glass of water. Refresh the water every few days; after a while, small roots will form. Pot the new plant, grouping three stems into one pot, and keep it inside in a warm, sunny place until the leaves have started to grow and it is more established. It can go outside if the weather is warm.

To Harvest

You can harvest lemongrass leaves at any time during its growing season to use fresh. Just cut off a leaf with scissors and use.

Make sure enough leaves remain on the plant so that it can continue to grow. Harvest a larger amount for drying when you cut back the leaves before the plant becomes dormant for the winter. Cut the leaves up into small pieces and lay them on a mesh screen or flat sieve. Set them somewhere warm to dry for twelve hours, or until completely dry (see page 259). Once totally dry

and crispy, store in a sealed glass container somewhere dry and dark until needed.

To Make Tea

Fill the kettle with fresh water. Bring the water to a boil, then pour some into your teacup to warm it up. Discard the water. Put three pinches of fresh or dried lemongrass leaves into a tea bag or teapot. Pour the boiled water (which should be between 176 to 185°F/80 to 85°C) over the tea and cover with a saucer or a lid to contain the aroma. Allow the tea to steep for three minutes. Remove the tea bag or pour the teapot using a tea strainer. Then enjoy a wonderful aromatic lemon tea. Lemongrass also makes a delicious iced tea. Steep the tea as before, then refrigerate until chilled. Serve with ice cubes and lemongrass leaves.

Tea Bag Friends

- For a tea to help with anxiety, blend lemongrass with violets. Put a pinch of each into a tea bag or teapot and pour on boiled water. Cover and steep for three minutes. Remove the tea bag or pour from a teapot using a tea strainer. Serve with a violet flower. Drink and enjoy.

- Blend lemongrass with calendula to aid digestion. Combine a pinch of calendula flowers and leaves and a pinch of lemongrass and steep as before.

TIPS

Lemongrass planted in your garden can act as an insect and snake repellent!

Warning: Lemongrass oil has been known to cause contact dermatitis, so handle with care.

Lemon Verbena

Aloysia triphylla

Lemon verbena is a highly scented perennial shrub with lovely bright green glossy leaves. It has small, pale lilac flowers in late summer and autumn. The plant originates from South America where there are over thirty species. *Aloysia* is part of the larger Verbenaceae family. *Triphylla* is the species name that describes the characteristic grouping of three leaves on the stem. In the past, it has been called *Aloysia citriodora*, referencing its lemon scent.

Medicinal Benefits

Lemon verbena tea is wonderful if you are detoxing, and it is a good tea to calm digestion and relax your body and mind. The leaves contain lemon-scented essential oil that helps the dried leaves retain their wonderful fresh lemon taste for many months. It promotes a good night's sleep and is also known to help clear cold symptoms and congestion. As with all teas, drink in moderation.

To Grow

Lemon verbena seeds need a warm climate to germinate. If you live in a more temperate climate you will need to buy a small lemon verbena plant to begin with. It ideally likes a sunny, sheltered spot and very well-drained soil. Under ideal warm conditions, it can grow to be 9 feet (3 meters) tall.

Lemon verbena can be grown in a container. In the early summer, repot your verbena into a larger pot to allow it room to grow. Make sure the pot has good drainage holes, and mix in some perlite or grit to further improve drainage. Feed your plant once a month during the spring and summer with an organic fertilizer such as liquid seaweed. If you would like to grow lemon verbena in your garden but the temperature in your area drops below 40°F (4°C) in the winter, plant it in a sheltered spot, mulch thickly around the roots, and cover the plant with a fleece during the colder months. If you live in an area that has frosts, it is a good idea to grow lemon verbena in a pot so that you can bring it inside when needed. If you have an unheated greenhouse, this would be an ideal place for the potted plant. It may lose its leaves quickly at this time. Do not overwater in the colder months, as it prefers to be kept on the dry side. The following spring, cut back the stems by a few inches to promote new growth.

Take cuttings in the spring or early summer when the fresh green shoots have grown and before it has flowered (see page 251). Cuttings wilt very quickly, so prepare your pot of soil before you take the cutting and water the cutting as soon as it is planted. Cuttings take a number of weeks to develop roots, but you should have a good sized plant to pot up and start harvesting the following summer.

To Harvest

Lemon verbena leaves can be harvested any time during its growing season. You can either pick off fresh leaves whenever you need them, or cut back the plant in late summer and dry many leaves in one go so that you have enough to last you the winter. To dry the leaves, spread them out on a flat sieve or baking sheet and leave them somewhere warm to dry for twenty-four hours. If you have many leaves to dry in one go, group the stems into bunches, tie them with a rubber band, and hang the bunches upside down in a warm place (see drying section page 259). When the leaves are totally dry, break them off of the stem, and store in a sealed glass container somewhere dry and dark until needed.

To Make Tea

Fill the kettle with fresh water. Bring the water to a boil, then pour some into your teacup or teapot to warm it up. Discard the water. Put three or four fresh or dried leaves into a tea bag or teapot. Pour the boiled water (which should be between 176 to 185°F/80 to 85°C) over the tea. Allow the tea to steep for three minutes. Remove the tea bag or pour the tea from the teapot using a tea strainer. You can add a fresh leaf to the cup before serving. The tea has a wonderful fresh lemony taste. Serve chilled and with ice cubes for a delicious iced tea in the summer.

Tea Bag Friends

- For a detox tea, blend lemon verbena with calendula. Put a pinch of each into a tea bag or teapot and steep as before. Remove the tea bag or strain from a teapot to serve. Drop a few fresh calendula petals in for decoration

- Lemon verbena is also lovely blended with black tea. Place some dried lemon verbena leaves in a sealed container with black tea leaves and allow the flavor to infuse over a few weeks.

TIPS

You can add lemon verbena leaves to many dishes in the kitchen, including steamed fish, or use it to make an amazing lemon verbena sorbet.

Warning: Lemon verbena can occasionally cause skin irritation when touched, as the leaves are slightly rough. Handle with gloves if your skin is sensitive.

Known to cause contact dermatitis, so handle with care

Manuka

Leptospermum scoparium

This large evergreen shrub is a native of New Zealand and Australia. A member of the Myrtaceae (myrtle) family, manuka has beautiful small white and pale pink fragrant flowers in the early summer, which the bees adore. There are many types of manuka, but this one can be identified by its small, pointed, dark green leaves, which are rather sharp to the touch. Early settlers to New Zealand made tea from this plant, hence its common name of tea tree. It makes the most delicious-tasting tea and you will be delighted to have discovered this new flavor.

Medicinal Benefits

The bees understand the importance of this plant and will eat nothing else if given the chance. The essential oils found in manuka are antibacterial, antiviral, antiseptic, and antifungal. Maoris have been using manuka for a variety of ailments for many years. It's an amazing plant to have in your garden, for your own well-being, but also for the bees!

To Grow

Manuka is an evergreen shrub that can grow to be 16 to 26 feet (5 to 8 meters) tall. It should be kept clipped and neat while the plant is small, otherwise it can become very woody and unruly. It likes well-drained soil, but water it well, as it does not tolerate drying out.

To grow manuka from seed you can get dried seedpods/capsules from another plant, allow the seeds to dry inside and wait a couple of days for them to open. Place the capsules in a sieve and shake it over a tray; the fine seeds will drop out. If you are starting with store-bought seeds, fill a seed tray with good quality seed compost mixed with 50 percent perlite or horticultural grit as manuka likes really good drainage. Lightly flatten the soil with a piece of wood or your fingers as the seeds are tiny. Sprinkle the seeds thinly over the soil. Sieve a fine layer of compost or sprinkle a thin covering of vermiculite or perlite over the seeds. Keep somewhere warm and sunny, and never let the seeds dry out. The seedlings will be tiny and slow growing. When they are about 1 inch (2.5 cm) tall, transplant them into pots of well-drained soil (see page 255). Always handle the seedlings by the leaf, as the roots do not like to be disturbed. I suggest growing some plants from seeds but also buying a plant to start off with, so that you can harvest some manuka to try in your first year.

If you start with a manuka plant, repot the plant into a larger pot every spring to encourage growth, until you reach the size of plant you desire. Clip the plant to keep it tidy and harvest the leaves for tea at the same time.

Manuka ideally likes to be planted in the ground in full sun and soil with good drainage. Try to plant it next to a lower-growing evergreen shrub, which will not only help shade its roots in the summer but will also shelter it from the wind. It likes a neutral or slightly acidic soil, so it is a good idea to mulch around your plant with bark. Once mature, the plants are frost hardy if planted in a sheltered position. Small plants, however, especially if they are in pots, may need frost protection if the temperature drops much below -5°F (-15°C). Bring the plant into an unheated greenhouse or conservatory or wrap the pot in bubble wrap or fleece, bringing the covering up the sides of the plant. Cover the whole plant with fleece, removing it during the day, until the frosts have passed. Manuka produces small woody seed capsules in the autumn, from which you can collect seeds to grow or share. You can take semi-ripe cuttings from late summer (see page 251). Cut ½ inch of bark off the base of the cutting on one side to help speed up rooting. Soak the cutting in water before planting and use at least 50 percent perlite or horticultural grit mixed with your potting soil.

To Harvest

It is best to harvest manuka when you are pruning the plant in the early spring. The stem and leaf can be used to make tea. Cut off the branches at the ends, trimming to keep a good shape and making sure you leave enough on the plant for it to keep growing happily. You will be able to harvest more each year. If you are harvesting in the summer, you can also use the flowers fresh or dried in your tea. Using scissors, cut the leaves and stems into very small pieces and use for a fresh manuka tea. To dry spread out the pieces on a tray or a fine sieve and place them somewhere warm to dry, moving the manuka around the tray every so often. Once the plant is totally dry and crispy, store in a sealed glass container in a dry and dark cupboard until needed.

To Make Tea

You can experiment with different amounts of manuka to suit your taste. Fill the kettle with fresh water. Bring the water to a boil, then pour some into your teacup or teapot to warm it up. Discard the water. Put one small teaspoon of manuka into a tea bag or teapot. Pour the boiled water (which should be between 176 to 185°F/80 to 85°C) over the tea and cover with a saucer or a lid. Allow the tea to steep for three to four minutes. Remove the tea bag or pour the tea from the teapot using a tea strainer.

There is little color to this tea but it has a strong and delicious flowery fragrant taste, so close your eyes and enjoy.

Tea Bag Friends

- Blend manuka (shown below on left) with saffron for a tea for good health. Put a pinch of manuka and a few strands of saffron into a tea bag or teapot. Cover and steep for three minutes. Remove the tea bag or strain the tea from the teapot and enjoy the flavorsome, aromatic tea.

- Blend a small pinch of manuka with crushed blueberries to give a slight fruit flavor to manuka tea. Infuse as before.

TIPS

- Kanuka (*Kunzea ericoides,* shown in photo on right) is another plant from the same family as manuka and looks very similar, but has a slightly larger, softer, and greener leaf. You can use kanuka for making tea in the same way as you do for manuka, so try and grow both plants if you have the space.

- You can try some manuka or kanuka leaves sprinkled on roast vegetables, or try smoking fish or meat using the fragrant sawdust from the stems.

- To confuse things, *Melaleuca alternifolia* is also commonly referred to as the tea tree plant. It is from the same family (Myrtaceae) as manuka but it has very different fluffy white flowers and cannot be used to make tea. Most Melaleuca are native to Australia.

Mint

Ginger mint *(Mentha x gracilis "Variegata")*

Strawberry mint *(Mentha "strawberry")*

Lavender mint *(Mentha "lavender")*

Spearmint *(Mentha spicata)*

Black peppermint *(Mentha x piperita)*

Garden mint *(Mentha sativa)*

Mints belong to the genus of plants called Mentha, which is part of the Lamiaceae family. There is an amazing selection of different flavors of mint, all of which make delicious flavorsome teas. They are herbaceous perennials, and will die back each year, but come up again the following spring. Generally, mints are very invasive, as the roots sprout new growth as they spread out from the plant. They are perfect to grow in pots in very small spaces, even on a windowsill. Some can grow up to 2½ feet (90 cm) tall. I have chosen six to show the range of colors and shapes of this plant. You can use any species or cultivar of Mentha to make tea, even though some plants are more medicinal than others. The flowers from the mint plant can also be used in the tea.

Medicinal Benefits

Mint is good for stomachaches and mild fevers. Peppermint is especially good for digestion and so is good to drink before a meal. Mint can also ease headaches and promote relaxation.

To Grow

You can easily buy seeds of many species of mint. Follow the specific instructions on the seed packet for each variety. It's easy to sow the seeds too thickly, so you may need to divide the seedlings when you transplant

them. Mint can be grown in a pot outside in a sunny or partially shaded spot. Water well and remove any dead or yellowing leaves. Repot into a larger container every year, or the roots will become jammed and have no space to grow. If necessary, split up your plants to give them more room. Remove the plant from the pot and use your hands to pull apart the roots. Divide it into as many separate plants as you want, making sure you leave yourself with a larger "stock" plant (see dividing page 255). Mints are very tough and can tolerate being separated in this way. Feed with a liq-

uid seaweed fertilizer once a year to keep the plant strong and healthy.

It is very easy to grow your mint from a cutting of a friend's plant, or from a bunch of mint from the grocery store. You may only get the common garden mint, but it is an inexpensive way to grow lots of mint plants. Cut a stem of mint to about 3 inches (8 cm) long and remove the lower leaves. Place it in a glass of water, which you should refresh every few days. The roots will grow easily in the water. When a large enough root has formed, the stem is ready to be potted. Fill a pot with potting soil, making a hole, and plant the cutting nice and deep. Keep it watered and somewhere warm and sheltered. It takes a few months for the plant to really become strong, but once it has, it will grow quickly. It can take over a garden, so think before you plant it directly into the ground. If you want to plant mint into the ground, I recommend leaving the pot on the plant. It sounds crazy, but it will help contain the plant's growth (although some roots will undoubtedly escape). As mints are perennial plants they tend to drop their leaves in the winter and the stalks are left looking untidy. Cut these off at the base of the plant, and the new growth will sprout from the bottom in the spring. Mints are frost hardy.

To Harvest

Harvest your plants from late spring to autumn. Harvest fresh leaves when you

need them, by pulling off the top of a stem. When you want to harvest more at one time to dry for storage, use scissors to cut off stems, leaving enough leaves on the plant for it to survive. It's a good time to neaten the plants' shape. Generally, cutting back the plant will make it become bushier, so in the long run your plant will look much better. Pluck off the leaves from the stem and spread them out on a flat sieve or rack or in a dehydrator (see page 260). When the leaves are dry and crispy, they are ready to be stored.

To Make Tea

Fill the kettle with fresh water. Bring the water to a boil, then pour some into your

- Mint blends well with many other plants in this book. I particularly like garden mint blended with blueberry for a tea to help your digestion. Put four dried and crushed blueberries into a tea bag or teapot with a pinch of mint leaves. Steep as before. Serve with fresh mint leaves.

- Try mint blended with a pinch of stevia, if you like a sweet mint taste.

- Mint is lovely in a sun tea blended with strawberries (see sun tea page 262).

TIPS

Mints are wonderful for use in the kitchen in salads, or in mint sauce or mint jelly to accompany lamb. My grandmother would never boil new potatoes or peas without putting in a sprig of mint.

teacup or teapot to warm it up. Discard the water. For a cup of fresh mint tea, you need about three or four fresh leaves per cup. This can depend on the variety and your taste, so experiment. You can put them straight into the cup, which looks lovely, or put the leaves into a tea bag or teapot. Pour the boiled water (which should be between 176 to 185°F/80 to 85°C) over the tea and cover with a saucer or a lid to keep the aroma trapped. Allow the tea to steep for three minutes. Remove the tea bag or pour the tea from the teapot using a tea strainer. Serve the tea with a fresh mint leaf or mint flower in the cup.

Mountain Pepper
Drimys lanceolata

M ountain pepper is an unusual plant with an amazing history. Its leaves and stems are highly aromatic, and it is a very attractive plant to grow.

Drimys (sometimes spelled *Drymis*) belongs to the Winteraceae family, native to South America and Australasia. They are believed to be a primitive plant, which originates from the ancient Gondwana supercontinent, millions of years ago. It is commonly known as mountain pepper or pepper leaf, because its seeds have been used as a pepper substitute. It is an evergreen shrub with long, slender, dark green leaves, with beautiful pinkish-red stems. It has small cream-colored flowers and pink buds in the late springtime. The flowers do not contain both male and female parts so you would need a male and a female plant in order to get fruit and seeds.

Drimys lanceolata is native to Australasia. To confuse matters further, it is also called *Tasmannia lanceolata* or *Drimys aromatica*. Another species, *Drimys winteri* (Winter's bark) or *canelo* in its native South America, can also be used to make a delicious aromatic tea. This species was named by Captain William Winter who, while traveling around the world with Sir Francis Drake, was given this plant by Native Americans, as a tea to treat his stomach sickness. It cured him, and he went on to give the tea to his ship's crew, as it is high in vitamin C and was a good defense against scurvy. *Drimys winteri* will grow into a tree and is thought to be less hardy than *Drimys lanceolata*.

Medicinal Benefits

Mountain pepper is thought to contain vitamin C, and also to have antifungal and antimicrobial properties. As with all plants, use with caution and do not use as an alternative to seeking medical advice.

To Grow

As this is an unusual plant, it may be harder to find than others in this book, but it is worth the search. Start off with the largest plant that you can find and afford, as it is slow growing. Plant in a sunny or semi-shaded spot, in moist, well-drained soil. It does not tolerate very cold winds, so plant it in a sheltered location if possible. In time it can grow into a beautiful evergreen hedge.

If necessary, keep your mountain pepper in a pot, repotting it every spring to give it room to grow and feeding it after repotting. Once it is established, you can take cuttings in the late summer or autumn (see page 251). If you live somewhere with winter temperatures below 23°F (-5°C), you can still grow this plant, but you will need to bring it into a greenhouse or conservatory for the winter months; or, if planted in the garden, protect the roots with mulch and totally cover the plant with a fleece.

To Harvest

Cut off a few leaves and the top of a stem as needed for a fresh cup of mountain pepper tea. Once it is established, you can harvest more leaves as you prune the plant in the autumn. Cut the harvested young stems up into small pieces and pluck off the leaves. To dry the plant place the leaves and stalks on a fine sieve or tray. Put in a warm place or in the oven at a low temperature, moving the plant around every so often. (See page 259.) Once completely dry and crispy store in a sealed glass container somewhere dry and dark until needed.

To Make Tea

Fill the kettle with fresh water. Bring the water to a boil, then pour some into your teacup or teapot to warm it up. Discard the water. Tear the mountain pepper leaves into small pieces and put two pinches (about five leaves with stems) of fresh mountain pepper in a tea bag or teapot. If you are using dried mountain pepper, add an extra pinch to your tea bag or pot, as mountain pepper is milder when dry. Pour the boiled water (which should be between 176 to 185°F/80 to 85°C) over the tea and cover with a saucer or a lid to contain the lovely aroma. Allow the tea to steep for four or five minutes.

Remove the tea bag or pour the tea from the teapot using a tea strainer. Drink and enjoy the gentle warm cinnamon smell and aromatic, slightly spicy flavor.

If you like a stronger flavor you can make a decoction by simmering the leaves and stems in a saucepan with 1½ cups of water for ten minutes. Strain and serve while hot.

Tea Bag Friends

- Mountain pepper is delicious blended with ginger, for a strong-tasting, health-boosting tea. Put two pinches of mountain pepper and one of ginger into a tea bag or teapot and steep as before.

- For a vitamin C boost, blend mountain pepper with rose hips. Put a pinch of rose hips and a pinch of mountain pepper into a saucepan with 1½ cups of water, cover, and simmer for ten to fifteen minutes to make a decoction. Strain and serve while hot. This is an aromatic, winter-warming tea.

TIPS

The leaves and black berries can be used as a spice in curries and stews.

New Jersey Tea
Ceanothus americanus

eanothus americanus is a deciduous shrub with an upright but compact habit. It is native to southern Canada and the central and eastern United States. It is an endangered species in the state of Maine, and wild plants should not be harvested. In New Jersey, when colonists needed a substitute for heavily taxed imported tea, they turned to an abundant native plant and gave it the name New Jersey tea.

New Jersey tea has oval, serrated leaves with leaf veins running the length of the leaf. It has long red roots, which give it its common name, red root. It was also called mountain snowbell or Indian tea before the American Revolution. It has delicate creamy white fragrant flowers in the summer. Bees, hummingbirds, and butterflies love *Ceanothus* nectar.

Medicinal Benefits

New Jersey tea was used by the Native Americans to treat fevers and sore throats. It is also thought to be good for bronchial complaints such as asthma, whooping cough, and tonsillitis.

To Grow

This is a lovely plant to have in a garden border. It grows to a maximum height of 3 feet (90 cm), so plant it toward the middle or front of a bed. In order to harvest this tea in your first year, buy a plant rather than growing from seed. New Jersey tea has a large root system so plant it in a deep container or in the garden. It needs well-drained soil and should be planted in a sunny or partly shaded spot. It is not a very thirsty plant and can withstand some mild drought conditions, but a severe drought can cause powdery mildew. The roots help to fix nitrogen in the soil, so it is a beneficial plant to have in your garden. Feed with liquid seaweed in the summer if growing it in a container. Take cuttings to make more plants in the late summer (see page 251). New Jersey tea is a hardy plant but it is deciduous, so it will lose its leaves and become dormant in the colder months. During this time, established plants can be dug up and divided to make more plants. However, the roots grow very deeply so it may be difficult to divide and move if the plant is very established. Prune lightly in the early spring and mulch with bark in the summer. If you cannot find *Ceaonothus americanus* you can also grow *Ceanothus velutinus*, commonly called tobacco brush. It is a much larger shrub, growing up to 13 feet (4 meters) tall, but will grow in similar conditions and can be used to make tea.

To Harvest

You can pick the leaves and young stems of the plant throughout the summer, making sure to leave enough leaves on the plant so that it can continue to grow. Use the leaves fresh or dry them for later use. Chop up the stems and spread the stems and leaves out on a mesh screen or tray to dry (see page 259), turning them every so often. Once totally dry and crispy, store in a sealed glass container somewhere dry and dark until needed.

To Make Tea

You can use New Jersey tea fresh from the plant or dry it for a stronger taste. Fill the kettle with fresh water. Bring the water to a boil, then pour some into your teacup or teapot to warm it up. Discard the water. Put about five fresh or dried leaves and stems into a tea bag or teapot. Pour the boiled water (which should be between 176 to 185°F/80 to 85°C) over the tea. Allow the tea to steep for three minutes. Remove the tea bag or pour the tea from the teapot using a tea strainer. Enjoy. This tea has a lovely pale yellow color and a taste similar to a very weak black tea.

Tea Bag Friends

Blend with myrtle for a great cough-defense tea. Put a pinch of myrtle berries and leaves and a pinch of New Jersey tea leaves into a tea bag or teapot and steep for 3 to 4 minutes. Remove the tea bag or pour the tea from the teapot using a tea strainer. Reuse the leaves for 2 or 3 subsequent cups.

TIPS

Rabbits and deer like to eat this *Ceanothus*, especially when the plant is young, so you may need to protect your plant with wire. The berries are not edible and should not be used for the tea. Other uses for the plant include making soap from the flowers and a red dye from its root. It has recently been found that the root contains a blood-clotting agent.

Raspberry
Rubus idaeus

Native to Europe, the raspberry is a sweet, soft, red fruit. You can make a delicious and nutritious tea from raspberry leaves, and the fruit can be dried to add to the leaf tea. The summer-fruiting (standard) variety produces a lot of fruit over a short period. Alternatively, autumn-fruiting or everbearing varieties will produce a smaller crop, but last from late summer until winter. Both will provide leaves that can be used for your tea. Find a variety suitable to your garden size, soil type, and local climate. Raspberry plants will continue to fruit for at least twelve years if maintained properly.

Medicinal Benefits

Raspberry leaves contain vitamins A, B, C, and E, calcium, and potassium. It is a very good antioxidant and can help ease menstrual cramps and relieve diarrhea. It can strengthen your immune system to relieve flu and cold symptoms and help ease sore throats. If you drink raspberry leaf tea during pregnancy, it is believed to help exercise the muscles of the uterus to ease labor. Always consult your doctor before taking this tea during pregnancy, as it is not advised in some cases.

To Grow

Raspberry plants are generally sold in the colder months when they are dormant, so don't be surprised if they arrive looking like sticks with roots on the bottom. The sticks are called canes and often come bare rooted (without pots). They are easy to find by mail order. Raspberry plants like rich, well-drained soil, so mix in lots of well-rotted manure or homemade garden compost. Plant 18 inches (45 cm) apart so that each plant has good ventilation and sunlight. Choose a sunny spot for them. If you are planting a summer-fruiting variety, you need to tie the plant to a wire support.

Autumn-fruiting varieties have a more compact, bushy shape. They produce fruit on one-year-old stems, so they do not require support and are suitable for growing in a container. They have shallow, wide-reaching roots, so make sure you have a large enough pot (15 inches/40 cm) or more in diameter) to accommodate them, and do not let them dry out. Autumn-fruiting raspberries will need to be pruned in late winter or early spring; all stems should be cut down to the ground.

Summer-fruiting raspberries fruit on two-year-old stems, so you need to prune them more carefully. In the autumn, cut any old, gray stems, which have already fruited, to ground level. Select about six of the strongest newly grown stems and tie them to a support with string. These are the stems that will bear fruit the following year. Cut down any other stems so that the plant is less crowded.

It is a good idea to mulch your raspberry plant with well-rotted manure or organic garden compost in the early spring, to feed the plant and help conserve moisture over the summer. Raspberries are susceptible to a number of pests and diseases so keep an eye on your plant and act quickly if you find anything. Cut back any diseased canes so as not to let it spread. Birds love to eat the fruit, so put netting over your plants to protect them if necessary.

To Harvest

Pick the youngest, freshest new leaves for a cup of fresh raspberry leaf tea. Check under the leaves for bugs such as whitefly, and wash off any you find. The plant should actually benefit from having some leaves removed as it will increase air ventilation and allow more sunlight to reach the plant. Remove the leaves from the stems. Harvest the fruits when totally ripe (you can pull them off their stalks easily).

TO DRY THE LEAVES

To speed up the drying process, cut up the leaves. Experiment with the size of the pieces, as it does affect the flavor. Spread out the leaves on a flat sieve or a baking tray and place in a warm room or near a warm radiator (see drying page 259). When the leaves are totally dry and crispy, transfer them to a sealed glass container and store in the dark until ready to use.

TO DRY THE FRUIT

As the fruit contain a lot of moisture, they take a long time to fully dry so need to be dried separately to the leaves. I found a dehydrator to be the most efficient way of drying raspberries as they retain their color and shape really well. Place the fruit on a dehydrator tray with the stem hole downward and dry them until hard.

dry, you can store the fruits (separately from the leaves) in a sealed glass container somewhere dry and dark until needed

To Make Tea

Fill the kettle with fresh water. Bring the water to a boil, then pour some into your teacup or teapot to warm it up. Discard the water. Put two pinches of fresh or dried raspberry leaves into a tea bag. Pour the boiled water (which should be between 176 to 185°F/80 to 85°C) over the tea. Allow the tea to steep for three minutes. Remove the tea bag (saving it for another cup) or pour the tea from the teapot using a tea strainer. Tea made from dried raspberry leaf will have a stronger taste and darker yellow color. It has a lovely depth of flavor not unlike an oolong tea. You can add

Alternatively, spread the fruit out on a baking sheet and place them in the oven set at a very low temperature of around 100°F (around 50°C) to dry for about 6 hours, turning them carefully every few hours. It is important that they are fully dry otherwise they will go moldy. The fruits should be very hard and light and should not be squeezable. If they are squeezable, dry them for longer. When sure they are

the fruit to the leaf to make a fruity-tasting tea. Crush the dried fruits in a mortar and pestle and put them into the tea bag or tea-pot with the raspberry leaf. Steep as before and serve with a couple of fresh raspberries in the cup.

Tea Bag Friends

- Try blending raspberry leaf with cardamom leaf. Put a pinch of raspberry leaf and a tiny pinch of cardamom into a tea bag or tea-pot. Steep and serve as before for a big-tasting delicious tea and a great defense against colds.

- Use fresh raspberries to make a sweet sun tea. Half fill a mason jar with fresh fruit and torn up fresh leaves and, add cold water, and close the lid. Leave in direct sun for up to five hours, stirring or shaking every so often. Then strain through a fine-mesh sieve or a ny-lon jelly bag (used for straining jams and jellies) and serve warm, or refrigerate and serve chilled with ice.

TIPS

Gargle with cold raspberry leaf tea to ease a sore throat.

Rosemary

Rosmarinus officinalis

"Miss Jessopp's Upright"

Rosemary is a Mediterranean herb, the flowers and leaves of which can be used to make tea. It is an evergreen shrub, with pointed narrow leaves and small mauve, pink, or sometimes white flowers that bloom in the spring and summer, depending on the variety. There are lots of cultivated varieties to choose from, including trailing varieties and low-growing varieties. I recommend "Miss Jessopp's Upright," as it is a lovely neat compact variety. Any *Rosmarinus officinalis* is suitable for making tea.

There is a lot of recorded history about rosemary. It has been used since the Middle Ages in bridal bouquets as a symbol of love and fidelity. In the fourteenth century, thieves were thought to be purged of the desire to steal when their feet were washed with rosemary. It is also a symbol of remembrance, and servicemen often carry a sprig to remember lost friendships. In Shakespeare's *Hamlet*, Ophelia says, "There's rosemary, that's for remembrance." It is still one of our most well-used and loved herbs.

Medicinal Benefits

Rosemary is antiseptic, anti-inflammatory, and a good antioxidant. It is believed to help with headaches, colds, and depression. It may stimulate the nervous system and circulation, and as a result may improve your memory. Rosemary tea is an energy-giving digestive tonic, and a great tea to keep you healthy.

To Grow

You can grow rosemary from seed but it is slow, and your plant may not grow true to its variety. Rosemary takes a few years to flower. If you buy a plant to begin with, you will be able to try rosemary tea in your first year. The plants are fairly easy to grow, as long as you do not overwater them. Rosemary can be grown in a container on a balcony or patio. As with all plants, increase the pot size as the plant grows. Use an organic potting soil or compost with a mix of grit or perlite to help improve the drainage (see page 250). Alternatively, rosemary can provide great structure to a flowerbed. It likes the sun, so choose a sunny location. It is a great companion plant in a vegetable garden as it may help keep away carrot fly and cabbage moths. "Miss Jessopp's Upright" is quite a woody variety, but regular harvesting for tea will keep the plant neat and bushy. It can even be shaped into a low hedge.

Certain varieties of rosemary can be sensitive to frosts, so they may need to be protected with a fleece or brought into an unheated greenhouse or similar space for the colder months. The easiest and cheapest way to get more rosemary plants is by taking cuttings (see page 251). In the late spring, take 4- to 6-inch (10 to 15 cm) long cuttings of new growth.

To Harvest

The flower tops are the most medicinal part of the rosemary plant, so harvest these to make tea. Make sure you only harvest leaves and flowers that have grown since you have been looking after the plant, to be sure no chemicals have been used on them. Strip the leaves and flowers from the woody stems. They are ready to be used for fresh rosemary tea or can be dried and stored for later use. To dry rosemary, spread out the leaves and flowers on a baking sheet and set them somewhere warm or dry them in a dehydrator (see page 260). When totally dry and crispy, store in a sealed glass container somewhere dry and dark until needed.

amazing aroma. Allow the tea to steep for three minutes. Remove the tea bag, or pour the tea from the teapot using a tea strainer, and enjoy. The tea has a pale yellow color, a delicious strong pine flavor, and a comforting, warming aroma.

Tea Bag Friends

- Saffron is amazing with rosemary. Put a pinch of rosemary and four or five strands of saffron into a tea bag and steep as before. This tea has a strong flavor and a strong yellow color.

- Blend with blueberries for healthy antioxidant tea. Put a pinch of rosemary with a pinch of crushed blueberries into a tea bag or teapot and pour on boiled water. Cover and infuse as before.

TIPS

Rosemary gives off its lovely aroma when it is burned on a grill or open fire. The perfect relaxing end to a summer evening.

Warning: Rosemary is not to be used by women who are pregnant or breastfeeding and should be used in moderation by all.

To Make Tea

Fill the kettle with fresh water. Bring the water to a boil, then pour some into your teacup or teapot to warm it up. Discard the water. Put a pinch of rosemary flowers and leaves into a tea bag or teapot. Pour the boiled water (which should be between 176 to 185°F/80 to 85°C) over the tea and cover with a saucer or a lid to trap the

Sage

Tangerine Sage *(Salvia elegans "Tangerine Sage")*

Pineapple Sage *(Salvia elegans "Scarlet Pineapple")*

For centuries, sage has been used by many cultures as a medicinal herb. Common sage (*Salvia officinalis*) can also be used as an infusion, and it is believed to have many medicinal properties. However, even though it is hardy and easier to grow than *S. elegans*, I find the taste a little overpowering, and prefer the fruit flavors of these two types. Pineapple sage has pointed, oval-shaped green leaves that smell strongly of pineapple. Tangerine sage has lovely rounded, heart-shaped green leaves. Both of these plants produce long, bright red, trumpet-shaped flowers in autumn and into early winter. Sage is loved by hummingbirds and bees.

Medicinal Benefits

The Romans believed that sage helped improve memory, heal infections, and cure snakebites! The word *salvia* comes from the Latin *salvere*, to save, so it is safe to say it is good for your general well-being.

To Grow

Start with a small plant, as this type of Salvia cannot be grown from seed. Tangerine and pineapple sage grow vigorously and can reach 3 to 4 feet (1 meter) tall in the right location and climate. It likes well-drained, moist soil and a warm, sheltered position. *Salvia elegans* is a semi-hardy perennial and can be killed off by hard frosts and temperatures lower than 5°F (-15°C). If you live in an area that experiences these low temperatures, you can either wrap your plant in fleece or bring the plant inside where it may even continue to flower. If it is planted in a garden, mulch around the base of the plant before the frosts arrive. You can grow this sage easily in a pot, and it can be kept inside all year around. Repot the plant into a larger pot every year to give it room to grow (see page 255). Cut back old stems in the early spring to promote new fresh growth. Water well and feed throughout the summer. It is easy to take softwood cuttings in the spring so that you have a supply of fresh young plants (see page 251). Sage is rabbit- and deer-proof, but slugs and snails like the small plants. Either set a beer trap nearby or lift the pots to uncover the culprits.

To Harvest

The flavor of the evergreen leaves will change depending on the time of year. Pluck leaves off as you need them or cut off larger stems to harvest many leaves in one go. Pick the flowers to accompany the leaves, as they retain their color and look beautiful.

To dry pineapple and tangerine sage, spread out the leaves and flowers on a fine-mesh flat sieve or baking sheet and set them somewhere warm and well ventilated to dry for twenty-four hours, or until totally dry (see page 261). Store in a sealed glass container somewhere dry and dark until needed.

To Make Tea

Fill the kettle with fresh water. Bring the water to a boil, then pour some into your teacup or teapot to warm it up. Discard the water. Put two pinches of fresh or dried sage leaves and flowers into a tea bag or teapot. Pour the boiled water (which should be between 176 to 185°F/80 to 85°C) over the tea and cover with a saucer or a lid. Allow the tea to steep for three minutes, then remove the tea bag or pour the tea from the teapot using a tea strainer. Enjoy. Add some fresh flowers for a striking cup of tea.

Sage tea is delicious iced and can be served with ice cubes and a slice of fresh pineapple or fresh orange.

Tea Bag Friends

- Blend pineapple or tangerine sage with lemon balm for a memory-boosting tea. Put a pinch of each into a tea bag or teapot and steep as before.

- Blend pineapple sage with fresh or dried lemon by simply placing a lemon slice in the tea cup to steep and then serve.

TIPS

You can also find blackcurrant sage (*Salvia microphylla* var. *microphylla*), which has smaller green leaves, but is equally good for making delicious tea.

Scented Pelargonium
(Scented Geranium)
Pelargonium

Scented pelargoniums, also called scented geraniums, are a tender perennial native to South Africa. There are many types of scented pelargonium with scents as varied as lavender, coconut, chocolate peppermint, cinnamon, cola, and black pepper. I have painted (clockwise from left): "Attar of Roses" top, which has a fragrant rose scent and mauve flowers, "Mabel Grey,"which has a glorious lemon scent and dark mauve flowers, the magnificent "Tomentosum," which has huge, velvety, peppermint flavored leaves with tiny white flowers and finally "Prince of Orange," which has a citrus orange scent and pale purple flowers. The flowers have a mild perfume in comparison to the incredibly strong scent of the leaves.

The Victorians loved scented pelargoniums and are thought to be responsible for the confusion in the misnaming of pelargoniums as geraniums. True geraniums are hardy herbaceous plants in the Geranium genus (not the Pelargonium genus). They are sometimes called hardy geraniums, or cranesbill.

I have chosen to use "scented geraniums" in the title of this chapter because "scented pelargoniums" are often incorrectly named as such. Standard garden pelargoniums and ivy-leaved pelargoniums are not scented, and are not suitable for making tea. If in doubt, search your supplier for "scented pelargoniums"!

Medicinal Benefits

Scented pelargonium is believed to be good for calming the body and relieving stress and anxiety. It is antibacterial so may help with stomachaches and diarrhea. It may also help with arthritis pain.

To Grow

Scented pelargoniums are generally an easy plant to grow. It is easiest and most reliable to start from small plants. There are some trailing varieties suitable for hanging baskets and some that are low-growing, so choose one suitable to your location. They do not like full sun all day, so if you live in a hot climate, plant them somewhere where they will be shaded for part of the day. They need four to five hours of sunlight a day and like an average temperature of about 70°F (21°C). They are tender perennials, so they will not survive a temperature below 40°F (5°C).

The easiest way to grow them, if you live where there are frosts, is in pots so that you can bring them into a greenhouse or a sunny spot in your own house for the winter. They are happy inside as a houseplant as long as they have enough light—otherwise, they may become leggy (spindly). You do not need to water them as much in the winter because the plant will become semi-dormant. If they do not have good ventilation, they can be susceptible to whitefly. Keep checking underneath the leaves, and if you find whitefly, immediately pinch off the infected leaves and discard them. You can also spray the plant with a garlic spray, if necessary. It is important to keep increasing the pot size to give the plant room to grow. Mix some perlite or fine grit into your potting soil or multipurpose compost to improve drainage. You should feed your geraniums an organic fertilizer such as seaweed once a month during the spring and summer. Deadhead the flowers when they have withered to help conserve the plant's energy. Pelargoniums are quick to grow from cuttings (see page 251). The cuttings need lots of light and like to be kept moist, but not soggy, as they can rot off. Do not cover the cuttings with a plastic bag.

To Harvest

You can harvest the leaves and flowers at any time during the warmer growing months. Harvest while you are pruning your plant, as this will keep it bushy and healthy. Look at your plant and cut off any stems that are too long or are out of shape. Pluck the leaves from the stems. They are ready to be used fresh or can be dried for later use. To dry the plant to use throughout the year, spread out the leaves on a flat sieve or baking sheet and place in a warm room or near a radiator. Alternatively, use a dehydrator (see page 260). When the plant is totally dry and crispy, store in a sealed glass container somewhere dry and dark until needed

To Make Tea

Fill the kettle with fresh water. Bring the water to a boil, then pour some into your teacup or teapot to warm it up. Discard the water. Put three or four fresh or dried pelargonium leaves and small parts of stalk into a tea bag or teapot. Tear the leaves into smaller pieces if they are large. Pour the boiled water (which should be between 176 to 185°F/80 to 85°C) over the tea and cover with a saucer or a lid. Allow the tea to steep for three to four minutes. (The leaves will discolor when the hot water is poured over them). Remove the tea bag or pour the tea from the teapot using a tea strainer and enjoy. You can also add a pelargonium flower before serving. The flavor will depend upon your type of pelargonium, but whichever you choose it will be a flavorsome and relaxing drink.

Scented pelargoniums make a lovely iced tea. Brew a larger amount as above and allow it to cool, then chill it in the refrigerator. Serve with pelargonium flowers frozen in ice cubes for a beautiful fragrant summer tea.

TIPS

You can put dried scented pelargonium into a cotton bag and leave it in a drawer to help keep moths away.

Warning: Some people may experience skin irritation when handling scented pelargoniums, so use with caution.

Tea Bag Friends

- Blend with black tea to create many different fragrant teas. Mix some dried scented pelargoniums into a sealed container of black tea. Keep it out of the light and allow the flavor to infuse over a few weeks. This makes a lovely present, too.

- Chamomile blended with lemon-scented pelargonium is a great calming tea to help with anxiety. Place a pinch of each into a tea bag or teapot and steep as before.

- For a stress-beating tea, blend tulsi with a lemon- or orange-scented pelargonium. Put a small pinch of tulsi and a larger pinch of scented pelargonium (one or two leaves) into a tea bag or tea pot and steep as before. An aromatic, warming, and feel-good tea.

Stevia

Stevia rebaudiana

Stevia is a tender shrub with long rounded leaves and small white flowers. It is also called sweet leaf or sugar leaf and is many times sweeter than normal sugar. This small shrub is a native of Paraguay, where it has been used by the indigenous population for hundreds of years. It was first processed into a food sweetener in Japan in 1971 and is now cultivated and processed in many countries.

Medicinal Benefits

Stevia can help with weight loss, as it contains no calories. It is an extremely useful sugar alternative for diabetics. As with all plants, use with caution and never use for a serious condition without first consulting your doctor.

To Grow

It is recommended to start growing stevia from a small plant or plug, as germinating the seeds can be slow and unreliable. Once established, the plants grow quickly but are tender and will not survive a temperature much lower than 40°F (4°C). Plant stevia in your garden in a sunny position. Dig up the plants and bring them inside during the cold months unless you live in a tropical climate. You can also grow stevia in pots so they are easier to bring inside in the winter. Place on a windowsill or somewhere warm with good light. They like rich, well-drained soil and need a lot of water, but they do not like to be waterlogged. Feed your stevia plants with an organic fertilizer, such as seaweed, every spring. They are susceptible to greenfly so mix up a garlic spray or buy an organic horticultural soap (see page 258) and keep an eye out for these pests. Slugs and

snails also love stevia so keep it out of their reach, if possible, and lay eggshells or grit around the base of your plant. The sweetness of the plant can diminish after three or four years so it is a good idea to take some cuttings in the early summer to get some new plants after this time.

To Harvest

The sweetness of stevia will vary and tends to be strongest later in the autumn before

the plant flowers and goes to seed. Remove the leaves from their stems and check that they are clear of insects. The leaves can be used fresh or can be dried for later use. If you are harvesting leaves to store for later months, cut off longer stems (about 5 inches long) and hang them upside down to dry for a week. Alternatively, remove the leaves from the thick stems and dry them on a baking sheet somewhere warm and well ventilated or in a dehydrator. Once totally dry and crispy, store in a sealed glass container somewhere dry and dark until needed.

To Make Tea

Stevia has a rather insignificant flavor, but an amazingly sweet aftertaste. Fill the kettle with fresh water. Bring the water to a boil, then pour some into your teacup or teapot to warm it up. Discard the water. Put five or six fresh or dried leaves into a tea bag or teapot. Dried stevia is stronger in color and flavor than fresh so vary the quantity according to your taste. Pour the boiled water (which should be between 176 to 185°F/80 to 85°C) over the tea and allow to steep for three to four minutes. Remove the tea bag or pour the tea from the tea pot using a tea strainer.

Tea Bag Friends

Stevia is best when it is used to sweeten other plants and can be used to sweeten any of the teas in this book. Mint, lemon balm, rose hip, and pineapple sage are especially good when mixed with stevia. Just add a pinch of stevia to the tea bag, teapot, or brewed decoction and steep as instructed before.

TIPS

There is a lot of research taking place into this plant so that its use as a food ingredient can be guaranteed as safe.

Sweet Tea Vine
Gynostemma pentaphyllum

Sweet tea vine is native to China and Southeast Asia and is also known as *jiaogulan* (pronounced JOW-goo-lawn), which means twisted vine in Chinese. In China, research was carried out into its use as an alternative sweetener, but scientists discovered something much more important. In the leaves, they found special compounds called saponins, known to benefit the immune system. There are many more saponins in *Gynostemma* than in ginseng, and it is often referred to as "poor man's ginseng." Sweet tea vine is a great tea to take as a body tonic for overall good health. It is known as the "immortality herb" and "miracle tea" because of the belief that it can prolong life and act as a cure-all. A census in China also revealed an area where there was an unusually high life expectancy, and it was found that the people there were regularly consuming *jiaogulan*.

Gynostemma is from the Cucurbitaceae family, which includes cucumbers and gourds. Its bright green leaves have serrated edges, covered in white hairs, and they can have up to five leaflets. It has tightly curled tendrils that help the plant to attach itself to nearby structures for support.

Medicinal Benefits

Gynostemma is used as a preventative herb to strengthen the immune system. Known as an adaptogenic herb by herbalists, it regulates the functions of the body to help keep a balance between the five systems: cardiovascular, digestive, immune, nervous, and reproductive.

It may help lower blood pressure and cholesterol and is believed to be a powerful antioxidant to help the body fight free radicals. It can increase energy levels and may help with stress, depression, and anxiety, as well as helping with jet lag. It contains many vitamins and minerals including calcium, iron, magnesium, zinc, potassium, and selenium. Use regularly to feel the full effects, but as with all the teas, consume in moderation.

To Grow

Sweet tea vine can be grown in the ground, up a wall trellis, or in a container.

Buy a plant early in the spring to start off and repot if necessary. Feed with an or-

ganic seaweed fertilizer if you are keeping it in a pot. If you are planting it in your garden, mix some sharp sand or horticultural grit into the soil to help improve drainage. It would also benefit from some seaweed granules being mixed into the soil. Even though it prefers well-drained soil, it also likes it roots to be kept moist, so water well throughout the summer. Place it in partial shade in hotter climates as the leaves can wilt quickly if it is too warm.

When the plant is small, its leaves will die off with a frost. If growing sweet tea vine in a container, protect it from frost by putting a few layers of horticultural fleece over the plant or bringing it inside into an unheated greenhouse or conservatory. Once established, the plant roots will be tolerant of temperatures as low as 0°F (-17°C). In frost-free areas it may grow all year round. Plants are either male or female, so you need to grow one of each in order for them to produce seeds. However, the climate and light levels may not be sufficient for them to produce flowers and seeds anyway. The easiest way to propagate sweet tea vine is to allow the plant stems to grow along the soil. These stems or runners will then produce roots that grow down into the soil. Once these are established, cut off the stem from the parent plant and pot the new plant in a mix of well-draining potting soil. It can become invasive, so grow in a container if you want to restrict it from spreading.

To Harvest

It is best to wait until your plant is really established, preferably more than two years old, before you harvest. Your plant should be well grown and ready to harvest in the summer months. Cut the number of leaves required at the base of the leaf, making sure enough remain so that the plant can continue to grow. If your plant is growing along the ground you may need to wash the leaves before use. Use the leaves fresh or dry them for later use. Lay the leaves on a baking tray or in a flat sieve and place in a

warm room or near a radiator turning every so often. Alternatively use a dehydrator. When totally dry and crispy, store in a sealed glass container somewhere dry and dark until needed.

To Make Tea

Fill the kettle with fresh water. Bring the water to a boil, then pour some into your teacup or teapot to warm it up. Discard the water. Put three fresh leaves or one pinch of dried sweet tea vine in a teacup or teapot. Pour the boiled water (which should be between 176 to 185°F/80 to 85°C) over the tea. Allow the tea to steep for three minutes, then remove the tea bag (and set it aside to use for subsequent cups) or pour the tea from the teapot using a tea strainer. You can put one fresh leaf in the cup to drink. The tea has a lovely mellow sweetness, similar to stevia, and a fresh green flavor, with a very slight bitter aftertaste. It is a lovely relaxing cup of tea.

Tea Bag Friends

• Blend with lavender for a general overall good health tea. Put a pinch of lavender flowers and a pinch of sweet tea vine leaves into a tea bag or teapot, cover, and steep as before.

• Blend with jasmine flowers for a possible antiaging tea. Put two pinches of sweet tea vine and a pinch of jasmine flowers into a tea bag or teapot, cover, and steep as before.

• Blend ginger with sweet tea vine for a body-balancing tea. Put a pinch of sweet tea vine and a small pinch of ginger into a tea bag or teapot, cover, and steep as before. This may be a good tea to help recovery after overexertion.

TIPS

You can use fresh sweet tea vine leaves in a salad.

Thyme

Lemon Curd Thyme *(Thymus serpyllum "Lemon Curd")*

Variegated Lemon Thyme *(Thymus x citriodorus "Variegatus")*

Orange Thyme *(Thymus citriodorus "Fragrantissimus")*

Thyme is native to southern Europe and was used by the Ancient Greeks and the Romans for medicinal purposes. It is an evergreen perennial with small rounded leaves, which are highly aromatic. It has small purple, pink, or white flowers, which the bees love. You can get upright or creeping varieties but I have chosen three that are lovely for making orange- or lemon-flavored tea.

Medicinal Benefits

Thyme contains essential oils and is known to be an antiseptic. It is good for colds and coughs and is believed to help fight phlegm and infections. It may help with stress and depression and it can help beat a hangover.

To Grow

You can start growing thyme from seed in the spring. Follow the instructions on the seed packet for your own particular variety. The seeds are tiny so they will only need a thin layer of potting soil sifted over them. They may not grow true to type from seed so it is best to start off with a small plant. Think of the Mediterranean to help understand the perfect conditions to grow thyme: well-drained, poor (low in nutrients) soil, and a sunny position. Pot in a mixture of 50 percent potting soil and 50 percent grit or perlite to create well-drained soil. Keep thyme on the dry side and water sparingly.

I have lost a lot of plants during wet, cold, and frosty weather, even though most species are listed as hardy. If you live in a cold climate, you may need to protect your thyme plants in the winter. Either cover them with a horticultural fleece, or move the plants inside an unheated greenhouse or somewhere that gets light but is protected from the frosts. Thyme can become very woody, so try to keep the plant trimmed back after it has flowered, using any green leaves from the trimmings for tea. In the springtime you can divide established plants. Dig them up and carefully pull apart the roots so you have smaller, but still good-sized plants to grow on.

To Harvest

You need a plant that is a few years old to really have enough foliage to use in the first year. By summer the plant should be full of lovely fresh leaves that are suitable for harvesting. Clip off some stems with scissors. Strip the leaves off the stems or cut up the very fresh stems to use as well. Use fresh, or dry on a mesh screen in a warm and well-ventilated place, on a tray in an oven or dehydrator (see page 259). When

completely dry and crispy store in a sealed glass container somewhere dry and dark until needed.

To Make Tea

Fresh thyme has more flavor than dried, so use it fresh in the warmer months when it is available. It has the most flavor before it has flowered.

Fill the kettle with fresh water. Bring the water to a boil, then pour some into your teacup or teapot to warm it up. Discard the water. Put three or four pinches of leaves into a tea bag or teapot and cover with a lid or a saucer to help contain the aroma. Pour the boiled water (which should be between 176 to 185°F/80 to 85°C) over the tea. Allow the tea to steep for three to four minutes. Remove the tea bag or pour the tea from the teapot using a tea strainer. It is

pale yellow in color with an aromatic lemon or orange flavor and makes a warming tea to drink on a cold night.

Tea Bag Friends

- Try sweetening this tea with stevia by placing one pinch of stevia in the tea bag or teapot along with the thyme.

- You can blend the aromatic taste of thyme with rose hips for a cough and cold defense. Strain a rose hip decoction into a teacup containing a tea bag of thyme and steep for 3 minutes, covering with a saucer to contain the aroma. Remove the tea bag and drink (see Rose Hip, page 162).

- Blend a pinch of thyme and a pinch of sweet tea vine for a hangover-relieving tea.

TIPS

There are many other types of thyme such as lavender, geranium, or mint, which also make wonderful teas.

Tulsi/Holy Basil

Ocimum tenuiflorum/Ocimum sanctum

Tulsi is native to Asia and has been used as a medicinal herb for thousands of years. For Hindus it represents the goddess Tulasi, who killed herself after being fooled into betraying her husband. It is a symbol of love, eternal life, and protection. It is grown in most Hindu households, as well as planted around sacred temples. It is also respected by many other religions and cultures.

Tulsi has a very strong taste of cloves with a hint of anise and mint. This species of basil is a perennial and can grow up to 3 feet (90 cm) tall. It has small pale pink flowers in the summer and oval-shaped, green, highly aromatic leaves.

Medicinal Benefits

Tulsi contains essential oils, the compounds of which hold many health benefits. It is believed to be antibacterial, antiseptic, and a great antioxidant. It may help improve digestion, lower a fever, and regulate your blood pressure. It helps fight off colds and flu and is believed to boost your immune system. It is also commonly used to relieve stress and tension.

To Grow

It is easiest to buy a tulsi plant in the spring. As the plant grows, keep repotting it into a slightly larger container each time. It likes nutrient-rich, well-drained sandy soil. Move plants outside during the summer months into a sunny and sheltered position. Feed every two weeks during the growing season with an organic fertilizer. If you like a challenge you can grow tulsi from seed but it is very slow and difficult to germinate. Plant the seeds inside from February onward (see page 253). Use a good seed-starting mix of 60 percent compost or seed-sowing compost and 40 percent perlite or sharp sand, if it is not already in the mix. Keep the soil moist but not saturated as they can easily rot if they are too wet.

Bring tulsi inside during the winter as they are tender and will not survive a frost. Place on a sunny windowsill where they can get lots of light, and do not overwater. In more temperate climates, low light levels in the winter may not be sufficient for tulsi to survive. You may have to treat it as an annual and buy a new plant every spring. If you live in a more tropical climate, tulsi is happy planted outside all year round in a sunny spot with moist soil. It is susceptible to whitefly, so keep an eye on the underside of the leaves. Squash any you see before they get a chance to multiply. You can also use a homemade garlic spray (see page 258).

To Harvest

Cut off the stems and pluck off the leaves, flowers, and soft stems. Use all these parts for a cup of fresh tulsi tea.

To dry tulsi, break stems into smaller pieces. Put the stems, leaves, and flowers on a tray or flat sieve in a warm room, near a radiator, in an oven or dehydrator (see page 260). When totally dry and crispy,

store in a sealed glass container somewhere dry and dark until needed.

To Make Tea

Fill the kettle with fresh water. Bring the water to a boil, then pour some into your teacup or teapot to warm it up. Discard the water. Put two pinches of fresh or dried tulsi leaves, flowers, and stems into a tea bag or teapot. Pour the boiled water (which should be between 176 to 185°F/80 to 85°C) over the tea. Allow the tea to steep for three minutes. Remove the tea bag or pour the tea from the teapot using a tea strainer and enjoy. Keep the leaves to make another cup. This is a really strong-tasting and reviving tea and a beautiful tea to make in a glass teapot. You can make tulsi into a refreshing iced tea in the summer. Make up a jug of tea by increasing the amount of tulsi according to the size of the container. Place in the fridge until chilled. Serve with ice and fresh tulsi flowers.

Tea Bag Friends

For a stress-beating tea, blend tulsi with a lemon- or orange-scented pelargonium. Put a small pinch of tulsi and a larger pinch of scented pelargonium (one or two leaves) into a tea bag or teapot and steep as before. An aromatic, warming, and feel-good tea.

Blend with a decoction of angelica for a tea to help digestion. Put a pinch of dried or fresh tulsi into a freshly made decoction of angelica (see angelica page 219). Allow the tulsi three minutes to infuse and then strain the tea through a tea strainer into a teacup.

TIPS

There are many other types of basil, such as cinnamon, lime, Greek basil, or sweet basil, that can be used to make tea. They do not have the same medicinal qualities as tulsi, but they have wonderful flavors.

SEEDS

Cilantro/Coriander

Coriandrum sativum

Cilantro is called coriander in the UK, and Chinese or Japanese parsley in Asia. It is a highly aromatic herb, used widely in cooking all over the world. It belongs to the Apaiceae or Umbelliferae family, which includes parsley, angelica, and fennel. It is an amazingly useful plant, as you can eat its shoots, leaves, flowers, seeds, and roots. It has a long recorded history, stretching back to the Bronze Age and possibly even earlier. It was found inside Tutankhamen's tomb, intended to accompany him to the afterlife. Cilantro was one of the first herbs to be planted by European colonists in North America in 1670.

It is an annual plant, so it completes its life cycle in a year, but it is a speedy annual and can grow flowers and come into seed very quickly. This is frustrating if you are only using the leaves, but great if you need the seeds. For tea, you primarily use the seeds (called coriander in the US), but the leaves add a depth of flavor. The seeds begin as lovely small, glossy, round green fruits that turn brown as they dry.

Medicinal Benefits

Cilantro has been used as a digestive aid for many years, by many different cultures. It may help the body to absorb nutrients and expel harmful toxins. It is an antibacterial plant, too, and has been used to help the body recover after food poisoning.

To Grow

You can buy small starter plants of coriander, but it is easy to grow from seed. It is easiest to sow the seeds directly into the ground, as cilantro does not like being transplanted. Plant in well-drained, moist soil in a partly shaded spot. Spread the seeds liberally over the soil and cover with about ¼ inch (1 cm) of soil. Keep sowing cilantro throughout the season so that you can have a continuous supply, as it is

a short-lived herb. You can grow cilantro in a pot as long as it is deep enough to accommodate its taproot (a minimum of 12 inches/30 cm). Water well, especially if growing it in a container.

To Harvest

Cilantro tea is best if it is a mix of seeds and leaves. The leaves become more feathery as the plant gets bigger, so you will need to

harvest them before this happens. Harvest the leaves and dry them at an earlier time than the seeds. Picking the leaves will prolong the life of the plant and delay it going to seed, too. Make sure you do not harvest too many leaves to allow the plant to continue to grow to produce its white flowers and then the seeds. It is best to let the seeds start to turn brown and dry out while still on the plant before you harvest them.

How you harvest cilantro will depend on how you want to dry it. You can cut long stems off if you would like to hang the seeds upside down to dry. Tie a small bunch with a rubber band to keep the herb bound as it dries and shrinks (see page 261). If you prefer to dry the seeds flat, pick them off of the stems once they have turned light brown and place them on a fine-mesh screen. The leaves can be left on their stems and dried whole. They keep a lovely green color when dried in a dehydrator. When totally dry, cilantro can be stored in a sealed container until needed. You can use the seeds when they are still green for a different-tasting cup of fresh cilantro tea.

To Make Tea

Fill the kettle with fresh water. Bring the water to a boil, then pour some into your teacup to warm it up. Discard the water. Grind about fifteen seeds in a mortar and pestle. Put the crushed seeds and two pinches of dried leaves into a tea bag or teapot. The leaves add a sweet flavor and turn the tea a lovely yellow color. The dried seeds have a strong lemony rose flavor. Pour the boiled water (which should be between 176 to 185°F/80 to 85°C) over the tea and cover with a saucer or a lid to retain the aroma. Allow the tea to steep for four minutes. Remove the tea bag or pour from the teapot using a tea strainer and enjoy this really relaxing aromatic tea.

Tea Bag Friends

- Try blending a pinch of cilantro seeds with a small pinch of fennel seeds for a strong digestive tea. Crush the seeds together in a mortar and pestle and then add them to your tea bag or teapot.

- To make a really delicious detox tea, blend two pinches of crushed cilantro seeds with a pinch of calendula.

- Try blending angelica with cilantro seeds. You can add a pinch of angelica root to a pinch of crushed cilantro seeds and brew them as a decoction (see Angelica, page 221). A great digestive tea.

TIPS

Cilantro may be susceptible to mildew if allowed to dry out, so keep an eye on your plants and remove any infected leaves immediately. Do not compost the diseased leaves.

Fennel
Foeniculum vulgare

ennel grows wild in many parts of Europe and North America, and it has been used widely as a medicinal herb for hundreds of years. The leaves and seeds can be used to make a wonderful aniseed-flavored tea. It is a perennial, which means that it lives for more than two years, but it will die back after it has gone to seed in the autumn. In addition to green fennel, you can find bronze fennel (*Foeniculum vulgare* "Purpureum") and a deep burgundy-colored fennel called *Foeniculum vulgare* "Rubrum," They are all suitable to use for fennel tea.

Medicinal Benefits

Fennel is an antioxidant and can calm your digestion and ease stomach problems. It can clear congestion associated with colds and sinus problems and may help lower blood pressure. It can reduce your appetite and therefore can help with weight loss.

To Grow

Fennel is easy to grow from seeds. Sow your seeds in the springtime when the weather has started to warm. You can start your seeds on a windowsill in small pots, or sow them directly outside in a garden or a deep container when the frosts have passed. If you have grown the seedlings inside, transplant them when the roots have just started to appear through the bottom of the tray or pot. Fennel likes to be planted in a sunny spot in well-drained and fertile soil. It does not like to be overwatered. Once you have a fennel plant established in your garden you can divide it to make more plants if you wish. You may find it self-seeds easily and new fennel plants can pop up all over your garden. Grow fennel in a large pot, a minimum of 12 inches (30 cm) deep, in order to contain the spread of this plant, and collect the seeds before they have a chance to drop.

To Harvest

The fennel plant has small umbrella-like arrangements of yellow flowers from late summertime to early fall. Allow the flowers petals to die off, leaving the tiny oval seed pods. These will turn from green to brown, with ridges along each seed.

When they are brown, place a paper bag over the seed head and hold it around the plant stem. Shake the dried flower head so that the seeds fall into the bag. Carefully

remove the bag, keeping your seeds inside, and pick off any seeds remaining on the flower head. Collect the seeds as each flower turns brown. Lay the seeds on a mesh or tray somewhere warm to make sure they are totally dry. Store the seeds in an airtight glass container in a dry, dark place and use as desired.

To Make Tea

Fill the kettle with fresh water. Bring the water to a boil, then pour some into your teacup or teapot to warm it up. Discard the water. Take a teaspoon or two pinches of dried fennel seeds and crush them in a mortar and pestle. Place the crushed seeds into an empty tea bag or teapot. Pour the boiled water (which should be between 176 to 185°F/80 to 85°C) over the tea and cover with a saucer or a lid to trap the aroma. Allow the tea to steep for three to four minutes. Remove the tea bag or pour the tea from the teapot using a tea strainer and enjoy!

If you want a cup of fennel tea before the seeds are dried and ready, you can use the fennel leaves. Take a large pinch of fresh young leaves and chop them up. Place them into a tea bag or teapot and steep as before. Enjoy this mild-tasting fennel tea.

Tea Bag Friends

- To make a great digestive tonic, blend fennel with licorice. Put a pinch of fennel seeds and a pinch of licorice root into a saucepan and add 1½ cups of water. Cover with a lid and simmer over low heat for ten to fifteen minutes. Strain through a tea strainer into a teacup. This is a strong and delicious tea. Reuse your licorice and fennel decoction for more than one cup.

- Try blending a pinch of cilantro seeds with a small pinch of fennel seeds for another digestive tea. Crush the seeds together in a mortar and pestle and then place them in a tea bag or teapot. Steep as before.

TIPS

Do not confuse this fennel with Florence fennel (*Foeniculum vulgare* var. *dulce*), which has a white bulb-shaped base and is eaten as a vegetable.

Warning: Do not be tempted to pick wild fennel as it looks similar to hemlock, which is highly poisonous.

Fenugreek

Trigonella foenum-graecum

enugreek is a medicinal plant used by the Romans and ancient Greeks. It is very popular in Asian cuisine, where is it called methi. Fenugreek is in the Leguminosae or Fabaceae family, to which peas and beans also belong. The seeds and leaves of the plant are used to make fenugreek tea. Depending on the variety, fenugreek can have yellow or white flowers, which grow into long, thin seedpods. Fenugreek is a spicy, powerful-smelling herb and the seeds are often used in curry powder.

Medicinal Benefits

The seeds contain protein, vitamin C, and potassium. They are good for your heart and may help to lower cholesterol. The leaves are high in protein, calcium, and iron. It is not recommended to use fenugreek while pregnant, but once the baby is born, it is known to help increase lactation for breast-feeding. Later in life, fenugreek may help women with the symptoms of menopause. For men, it may help with hair loss and may also be an aphrodisiac.

To Grow

It is easy to start fenugreek from seed, as it is a fast-growing annual. You can buy large packets of fenugreek seed from the grocery store, in the spice department. This variety has small white flowers. Fenugreek is best sown directly outside once it is warm, into a prepared bed of well-drained soil. Scatter the seeds over the soil and cover with a sprinkling of soil. Germination is very quick and easy. Fenugreek can be grown in a container as long as it is deep enough (12 inches/30 cm). Once the seedlings have grown to about 2 inches (5 cm) tall they need to be thinned to give each plant room to grow. This is the time to harvest the leaves to be used for tea. The plants need about 3 inches (7 cm) of space between them in order to grow big enough to produce seeds.

Fenugreek is fairly drought tolerant once the plants are established. It grows rapidly and will go to seed by the late summer if sown in the spring. By growing your own seeds and leaves you can be sure that they are safe and free from chemicals. Slugs and snails will eat lots of the smaller fenugreek shoots so keep lifting up your pots to make sure none are hiding beneath. Put the plants somewhere less accessible to these pests, lay eggshells around your plants, or set a beer trap (see page 258).

dry, put the seeds in a sealed glass container and store in a dry dark location ready to be used with the dried leaves for a nutritious fenugreek tea.

To Make Tea

Fill the kettle with fresh water. Bring the water to a boil, then pour some into your teacup or teapot to warm it up. Discard the water. Put a large pinch of seeds and a pinch of dried fenugreek leaves into a tea bag or teapot. Pour the boiled water (which should be between 176 to 185°F/80 to 85°C) over the tea. Allow the tea to steep for three minutes. Remove the tea bag or

To Harvest

You will need to harvest the seeds and the leaves at separate times, to get the best ingredients for your tea. Earlier on the season, when you are thinning the seedlings in the early summer, you should harvest leaves. Dry the leaves (see page 259) and store them in a sealed glass container in the dark. Long green seedpods will develop on the remaining plants and should be left on the plant to ripen. Pick the seedpods when they have turned a light brown but before they open. Each seedpod contains many seeds, so collect these in a bowl. Place on a tray and put in a warm room. When totally

pour the tea from the teapot using a tea strainer. The seeds create very yellow tea with a strong, sweet curry smell. It has a fresh bean taste and a sweet maple syrup flavor. This tea creates a relaxing and calming effect on the body.

Tea Bag Friends

- Blend with blueberry for a possibly cholesterol-lowering tea. Put five crushed dried blueberries and a pinch of dried fenugreek leaves and seeds into a tea bag or teapot and steep for 3 to 4 minutes.

- Blend with coriander seeds and leaves. Crush a pinch of coriander seeds and add to a pinch of fenugreek seeds and a pinch of dried or fresh coriander leaves. Put in a tea bag or into a teapot and pour on boiled water as before.

TIPS

Fenugreek is used to flavor fake maple syrup!

Warning: Not to be used by pregnant women as it may cause premature labor.

FRUITS

Blueberry
Vaccinium corymbosum

Native to North America, the blueberry is now a popular garden plant across the world. You can get evergreen blueberries, but *Vaccinium corymbosum* is a deciduous shrub. It will lose its leaves in the winter, after they turn a stunning red color in the fall. They have lovely white, sometimes pinkish flowers, which develop into fruit in midsummer or early autumn. Blueberry plants will bear fruit for many years and each year will hopefully reward you with a bigger crop than the last.

Nutritional Benefits

It is well known how good blueberries are for us. They are high in anti-oxidants, vitamin C, vitamin A, and vitamin E. They can help boost your immune system, sustain your eyesight, help lower cholesterol, and improve digestion. They may help with memory loss and can improve brain function and learning capacity.

To Grow

There are many cultivated blueberry varieties to choose from, and a very popular one is *Vaccinium corymbosum*, or high-bush blueberry. Try to buy two- or three-year-old plants so that you will have some fruit in your first year. Choose the hardiest variety for your location so you do not have to worry about winter protection. There

is another cultivated variety called rabbit-eye blueberries (*Vaccinium ashei*) that bear smaller fruits, similar to wild blueberries, but are easier to grow than other high-bush varieties.

If you have space, grow two or more varieties. Blueberry flowers have both male and female organs but they cannot be fertilized by their own pollen. Having other varieties close by will help the bees and ensure you get a bigger crop of fruit. Blueberries like an acidic soil, and the pH needs to be below 5.5 for most blueberries to thrive. You can buy simple pH test kits cheaply from garden centers to test your plot. If your soil is not acidic, it is easiest to grow blueberries in a container. Use ericaceous soil or acidic compost, which is for acid-loving plants. Try and find a low-peat version or one that uses pine bark instead of peat if possible, as peat extraction is very bad environmentally. Make sure your pot has drainage holes and crocks (broken bits of pot) in the bottom to help improve drainage. Blueberries like well-drained but moist soil, and a sunny or partly shaded, sheltered position. They love to be given rainwater to drink, as it is more acidic than tap water. To feed the plant, put a layer of homemade organic compost from your composter or wormery around the plant covering with a layer of bark chipping mulch to help retain moisture.

When the fruits have formed and are starting to turn color, you should cover your blueberry with a net to stop the birds from eating your harvest. Position four canes in the ground around the plant and attach a fine net to these using clothes pegs or string.

Prune your blueberry plants in the winter to neaten them up and to promote new growth the following year. Cut any dead stems to the base and the brown ends of the stems to the closest growing buds. Cut any stems that have fruited that year down to ground level. If container grown, they will need repotting into a larger pot in the spring. Use ericaceous/acidic potting soil as before. You can take cuttings in the spring to make more plants (see page 251). Make sure you use ericaceous or acidic compost for the cuttings.

To Harvest

Pick your blueberries when they are ripe but still firm. Use them fresh or dry the berries using a dehydrator or an oven (see page 260). As blueberries have a protective skin and are very juicy, they need to be either blanched or pricked before they are

dried. To blanch the fruit, place the blue-berries in a metal sieve and dip them into a saucepan of boiling water for a few seconds (you don't want the skins to burst), then immediately plunge them into cold water. This should soften the skins to help speed up the drying process, which will take about twenty-two hours in a dehydrator. I find the most efficient way was to prick each berry about ten times with a pin. This significantly reduces the drying time need-ed (about seventeen hours) but obviously takes longer to prepare than blanching.

To Make Tea

Fill the kettle with fresh water. Bring the water to a boil, then pour some into your teacup or teapot to warm it up. Discard the

water. For a cup of fresh blueberry tea, put about seven berries (or more, if you like a stronger taste) into a tea bag or teapot. For a cup of dried blueberry tea, you need to grind the berries. Put seven berries into a mortar and pestle and grind until broken up. Put the ground blueberries into a tea bag or teapot. Pour the boiled water (which should be between 176 to 185°F/80 to 85°C) over the tea. Allow the tea to steep for four minutes, lifting the bag up and down to help extract the flavor or stirring if you are using a teapot. Remove the tea bag or pour the tea from the teapot using a tea strainer. The tea is a lovely deep red color and has a refreshing fruity taste.

Tea Bag Friends

- Blend with hyssop for an antioxidant-boosting tea. Put two pinches of ground blueberry and a small pinch of dried or fresh hyssop leaves into a tea bag or teapot and steep for three to four minutes. Serve with fresh hyssop flowers.

- Blend a small pinch of fresh or dried manuka with crushed blueberries to give a slight fruit flavor to this aromatic tea.

TIPS

Blueberries belong to the same genus (*Vaccinium*) as cranberries, bilberries, huckleberries, and lingonberries. There are about 450 species of plants in this genus.

Lemon

Citrus x limon

emons were introduced to Europe over 1,000 years ago. Christopher Columbus is believed to have brought the first lemons to America in the fifteenth century, and Italy and the US are now the biggest producers of lemons in the world. Lemons are used for a huge range of foods and products. Lemon trees have dark green, oval-shaped leaves, and beautifully scented white flowers that grow into fruit.

A lemon grown from a seed will not produce identical lemons as its parent tree, and the plant may take about ten years to fruit. So commercially, to speed up fruiting and to ensure the quality of the fruit produced, citrus trees are often grafted. To graft a plant, a section of stem containing a leaf bud (called a scion) is placed into the stem of another plant (called the stock). The two parts join and grow together into a new plant. Although more expensive to buy initially because of the work that has been involved in their development, grafted trees will give better quality fruit in a shorter amount of time. The good news is that they are self-fertile so you only need one lemon plant to obtain fruit.

Medicinal Benefits

Lemons contain high levels of vitamin C, as well as calcium, vitamin B, and niacin. They are used as an antibacterial and antiviral fruit, so they are a great defense against colds and flu.

To Grow

In order to have lemons to use for making tea I advise buying a grafted lemon plant. They can be grown outside in a sheltered position if you live in a frost-free climate where the temperature does not fall below 44°F (7 °C). They can reach 10 to 20 feet (3 to 6 meters) tall if the conditions are ideal. If your climate has low winter temperatures, they should be grown in a pot outside in the summer and moved inside during the colder months. To successfully grow a lemon inside, it is vital to choose the right position for it. These are the main factors to consider:

Light
Lemon plants need lots of light, so a conservatory or greenhouse is perfect.

Temperature
Lemon plants like to be a constant cool (not cold) temperature. They will not tolerate being near a radiator or in a drafty place.

Water
Lemon plants like to be given rainwater, if possible. Give it a good amount until you can see the water draining from the holes in the bottom of the pot. Then allow the plant to become fairly dry before the next watering, but be careful not to let it dry out completely. It does not like to be overwatered so don't water the plant more than once a week in the winter months. When your lemon starts to flower, it is critical that you have a regular watering routine established, otherwise the flowers will drop. It can take a year for a flower to fully develop into a fruit.

Humidity
Lemon plants like to have their leaves sprayed with water every so often. In the warmer months, you can stand the pot on stones set in a saucer of water to help increase the humidity around the plant.

Repot the lemon plant in the spring every couple of years using good organic potting soil mixed with fine bark to improve drainage and to make the compost more acidic. Your plants will enjoy being outside in the summer months, and the fresh air will help to keep pests and diseases away. Lemons are hungry plants and will need to be fed with an organic citrus plant food or liquid seaweed. Be careful when you are handling your lemon plant as it may have sharp thorns.

You can grow lemons from pips as long as you are prepared to wait a long time for the fruit. It is great fun to try, and you will really gain an understanding of how to care for your lemon tree. Sow lemon seeds or pips straight after you have taken them out of the lemon. Plant seeds ¼ inch (1 cm) deep in good quality potting soil and keep the seeds in a warm and light place. Water as before. Good luck!

To Harvest

When your lemons are yellow, they are ripe and ready to pick. Pick them as you need them, leaving any others on the plant. If you have a lot of lemons ready at the same time you can dry some to use at other times of the year (see page 260). Cut slices of similar thickness and dry them in the oven for about six hours, turning the slices over every half hour. To dry in a dehydra-

tor, dry at 130°F (55°C) for twelve to twenty hours, until brittle. They look more like oranges when they are dried but still retain their delicious lemon taste. When they are totally dry and hard they can be stored in a sealed glass container, somewhere dry and dark until needed.

To Make Tea

Fill the kettle with fresh water. Bring the water to a boil, then pour some into your teacup or teapot to warm it up. Discard the water. Put two slices of fresh lemon into a teacup or teapot. If using dried lemons, one slice will probably be sufficient, as their flavor is stronger. Pour the boiled water (which should be between 176 to 185°F/80

to 85°C) over the lemon slices. Cover with a saucer or lid. Allow the tea to steep for three minutes, remove the lid and then relax and enjoy. This makes a wonderful iced tea or sun tea (see page 262).

Tea Bag Friends

- Lemon can be blended with many other teas including black tea, mint, and echinacea. Simply add a slice of fresh or dried lemon to the final cup of tea and allow to infuse for three minutes. Leave the lemon in the cup to drink.

- Blend with stevia to sweeten, if necessary.

TIPS

Lemon juice can also be used as a stain remover.

Myrtle
Myrtus communis

This evergreen shrub is often called common myrtle. It has densely packed, aromatic, glossy leaves and has white flowers in the summer, followed by a profusion of glossy black berries in the winter. It is thought to be native to Europe, particularly the Mediterranean, and to western Asia. It is from the Myrtaceae family, to which manuka also belongs. Myrtle has long been an important symbolic and medicinal plant. Venus, the Roman goddess of love and beauty, wore a crown of myrtle, and it is a symbol of love and fidelity. Queen Elizabeth II had a sprig of myrtle in her wedding bouquet taken from the same plant that was used in Queen Victoria's. It is also an important plant in the Jewish religion and represents immortality during the sukkah ceremony.

There are some cultivated varieties of the *Myrtus communis* species, such as *Myrtus communis* "Microphylla," which has a compact growing habit and small leaves. *Myrtus communis* "Variegata" is a variegated leaf variety.

Medicinal Benefits

Myrtle contains essential oils believed to be anti-inflammatory and antibacterial. It is thought to be good for bronchial complaints and coughs, as well as digestive problems. It is also believed to help with sinus infections.

To Grow

You should think about the Mediterranean when planting and growing your myrtle. It likes full sun and well-drained soil. Try to buy a two- or three-year-old plant to begin with (it will need to be in a pot at least 6 inches (15 cm) across). Myrtle is easy to look after once it is established. Plant your myrtle in a sheltered place, next to a wall or protected by other shrubs. It is not frost hardy in an exposed site if the temperature drops below 5°F (-15°C). In the winter, you can protect your myrtle with horticultural fleece or bring it into an unheated greenhouse or a cool, sunny room inside your house. If your climate is warm enough, myrtle will be happy outside all year round. It can grow into a wonderful dense and aromatic hedge up to 16 feet (5 meters) tall but can also be grown in a container. Repot it every spring to give it room to grow. Use an organic peat-free potting soil or compost, mixed with a little grit, to improve drainage. Water enough to keep the soil moist but not soggy. Feed in the spring with an organic fertilizer. Propagate by semi-hardwood cuttings in late summer.

To Harvest

Once the plant is established, you should be rewarded with lots of glossy black berries, which can be harvested throughout the winter. As the plant is evergreen, the leaves can be picked whenever you need them. The berries take two days to dry on a low radiator but take less time if you first prick them with a pin. It is best to dry them in a low oven or in a dehydrator (see page 260). Dry the leaves separately, as they

of berries and leaves in myrtle tea. Put five or six fresh or dried berries and a pinch of broken leaves into a tea bag or teapot. Pour the boiled water (which should be between 176 to 185°F/80 to 85°C) over the tea. Allow the tea to steep for three to four minutes Remove the tea bag or pour the tea from the teapot using a tea strainer then enjoy. You can make a decoction of this tea if you would like a stronger flavor. Put the myrtle leaves and berries into a small saucepan and add 1½ cups of water. Cover and simmer for ten to fifteen minutes. Strain through a tea strainer and drink hot.

take less time than the berries. When completely dry store the berries and the leaves separately in sealed glass containers, somewhere dry and dark until needed.

To Make Tea

Myrtle has a strong aroma and a taste that reminds me of eucalyptus. You should tear the fresh leaves or break up the dried leaves to help release their flavor before using. It is a great tea to have in the winter, when the berries are on the plant.

Fill the kettle with fresh water. Bring the water to a boil, then pour some into your teacup or teapot to warm it up. Discard the water. I like using a combination

Tea Bag Friends

- Blend myrtle with rose hips in a decoction for a cough and cold defense. Add 1½ cups of water to a pinch of rose hips and four myrtle berries and a pinch of broken myrtle leaves into a saucepan. Bring to the boil and then simmer gently. After ten to fifteen minutes, strain the tea and serve hot. This is a very soothing, warming cup of tea.

- Blend with violet for an anti-inflammatory tea. Make a decoction of myrtle as above and then infuse some violet leaves and flowers into it. Allow to steep for three minutes, then strain into a teacup and enjoy.

TIPS

- The berries are sweet to eat but have large bitter seeds. The leaves and fruits are great to use in stews and other meat or fish dishes.

- Lemon myrtle (*Backhousia citriodora*) is from the Myrtaceae family but is from a different genus (Backhousia). It is also suitable for making tea.

- Make sure you use the Latin name when finding your plants. There are other, unrelated plants that are commonly called myrtle but are not suitable for making tea.

Rose Hip

Rosa rugosa

Rose hips are the fruits of a rose plant. Rose hips form after bees have pollinated the rose flower, so it is important not to remove the dead flower heads from your rose bushes if you want beautiful rose hips to develop and ripen. Not all roses produce hips, as a lot of roses are bred to have tightly packed petal formations and as a result, pollinating insects are unable to access the flower.

Medicinal Benefits

There is about twenty times more vitamin C in rose hips than there is in oranges. Vitamin C helps maintain a healthy immune system and can prevent colds and flu. Rose hips also contain vitamin E, vitamin B1, calcium, and magnesium as well as flavonoids (antioxidants). They are also used as an anti-inflammatory and can help reduce the pain of arthritis.

To Grow

Rosa rugosa produce large, round, reddish orange hips that have a tangy, fruity flavor. Specific recommended varieties to choose are Rosa rugosa "Rubra" or *Rosa rugosa* "Alba." If you buy your rose from a garden center, it is likely to be in a pot. If you buy roses by mail order they are often cheaper, but will arrive bare rooted, without a pot. This is fine, as they travel safely like this, but they must be potted and watered as soon as you receive them.

Read the label of the rose you have selected and plant it in an appropriate position in the ground or in a container. Soak the rose in a bucket of water for ten minutes. Roses need well-fertilized soil, so mix some bonemeal or homemade compost into the existing soil where the rose is to be planted. They can be planted in a sunny or partly shaded location. Dig a hole in the ground about twice as wide as the plant's roots. Unwrap the rose or take it out of its pot and tease open the roots to help it get established quickly. Place the rose into the hole, making sure the branches remain above the soil level. Fill around the plant with soil and compact the soil with your boot. Water well.

If you would like to grow your rose in a pot, find a pot about twice as large as the size of the root. Use a good quality organic potting soil with sharp sand or grit mixed in to improve drainage. Take the rose out of its bag or pot and tease out the roots, and then lower the rose into the (new) pot. Fill around the plant with soil, pushing the soil downward with your fingers. Stand the plant somewhere sunny and repot it every year or when its roots have filled up the pot. Water well and never let the soil dry out.

Feed your rose every spring with an organic fertilizer. Depending on the species of rose, it may need pruning in the spring to encourage new growth and flowers. Follow the specific instructions on your rose.

To Harvest

Pick your rose hips when they are round and brightly colored. This is normally in the fall, so you should pick enough to last you for many months. Cut the hips off of the plant and place them in a basket. You can use the hips fresh or dry them for later use. Cut off the bottom stem and also the dark furry tops of the hips. To dry lots of fruit, put the "topped-and-tailed" hips in a food processor and pulse to grind them a little—but not too much! Spread the chopped hips on a baking sheet and put into a warm oven on the lowest temperature setting. Move the hips around the tray every five minutes while they are drying.

They should take about twenty minutes. When they are dry, tip them into a sieve and shake all the tiny hairs out. These are what itching powder is made from. They have been known to cause minor irritation for some people, but I have never experienced this. If you are worried, you can be more thorough by cutting the hips in half and scraping out the hairs with a teaspoon before you put them into the food processor. When the hips are a darker color and are totally dry and hard they can be stored in a sealed glass container somewhere dry and dark until needed.

To Make Tea

To make fresh rose hip tea, snap the stems off each hip and then remove the dark furry top of each hip with a knife. Cut four hips in half and remove the seeds and hairs with a teaspoon. Place them in a small saucepan with 1½ cups of water and simmer for ten to fifteen minutes. Strain into a teacup and enjoy a gently flavored cup of fresh rose hip tea. For a stronger taste, use dried rose hips. Place 1 teaspoon of dried rose hips

• Rose hips are delicious when blended with mountain pepper for a vitamin C boost. Put a pinch of rose hips and a pinch of mountain pepper into a pan with 1½ cups of water, cover, and simmer for ten to fifteen minutes. Strain into a teacup and serve hot. This is an aromatic, winter warming tea.

• You can blend the aromatic taste of thyme with rose hips for a cough and cold defense. Make a decoction of rose hips as above and then pour into a teacup with a tea bag or teapot containing a pinch of thyme. After three minutes remove the tea bag or pour the tea from the teapot using a tea strainer.

TIPS

Do not use any rose hips that you have not grown yourself as they may have been sprayed with chemicals.

in a saucepan with 1½ cups of water, cover, and simmer for ten to fifteen minutes. Strain into a teacup and serve hot. This is a deliciously sweet, almost caramel-tasting tea to help keep colds away.

Strawberry

Fragaria

Strawberries originate from the wild strawberry (*Fragaria vesca*), which is native to Eurasia and North America. Humans have been eating strawberries since the Stone Age. They have been cultivated since the sixteenth century and over time we have created bigger, sweeter, and more colorful varieties.

There are hundreds of varieties of strawberries, so choose one suitable to your location and climate. There are three main types: "June-bearing," "everbearing," and "day-neutral" varieties. June-bearing, or "summer bearers," yield the largest fruits over a short period of time. They are divided further into Early Season, Mid Season, and Late Season. "Everbearing," "Alpine," or "Wild" strawberries can produce very small fruit twice a year, once in the spring and again in the late summer. They do not tend to produce runners like the June-bearing varieties. Day-neutral or "perpetual" varieties produce lots of fruit over a long period of warm weather, but the fruit can be smaller than June-bearing varieties. Strawberry leaves, stems, flowers, and fruit can all be used to make tea.

Medicinal Benefits

Homegrown strawberries are very nutritious and contain lots of vitamin C, potassium, and calcium. Strawberries are believed to help with fevers, infections, fainting, and depression. They are an antioxidant and can help the liver as well as help alleviate digestive problems.

To Grow

Strawberry seeds can be slow to germinate, so I recommend starting off with small plants. It is ideal to buy your strawberry plants in the early spring so you have the full growing season ahead of you. Don't plant strawberries where you previously planted potatoes, peppers, or tomatoes, as these can harbor disease within the soil. Strawberries need full sun and well-drained soil. They also need a fairly sheltered position so that bees and insects can easily pollinate the flowers. Mix some homemade compost or other humus into the soil where the strawberries are to be planted. Make a hole and place the plant so that the crown (the part from which the stems are growing) is at the same level as the earth. You can plant in a mound of soil to help raise the crown to the correct level. Use a mulch of straw around the plants, to help prevent slug damage and to keep the fruit clean and dry. Water well, especially when the fruits are ripening. Keep the area around your strawberries free of weeds so they do not take any goodness away from your plants. Strawberries will flower in the spring. If a late spring frost is forecast and your strawberries have flowers on them, place a horticultural fleece or light sheet over the plants for the night. Remove it the next morning or when the frost has passed. If the frost kills the flowers, you will not get any strawberries.

Feed your plants once a month throughout the summer with an organic fertilizer such as seaweed or bonemeal. If birds are stealing your fruit, cover your strawberries with netting. Growing strawberries in containers helps to keep the slugs away. Make sure you fill your container with enough potting soil that the strawberry crown is level with the top of the container, so that when the fruit form they can hang over the edge. They do well in hanging baskets as long as they are given enough water. If you live in a cold climate and the temperature drops below 5°F (-15°C), you should cover your strawberry plants with 4 to 6 inches of straw for the winter. Clear off the straw in the spring so the plants can begin growing again. You are encouraged to remove the first year's flowers to promote a bumper crop in the second year, but I have never managed to bring myself to do this! Most strawberry plants produce runners or stolons, which are long stems that grow out and away from the plant. New baby plants develop along the runners, and when they come in contact with the earth, roots grow. These can be separated from the parent plant and potted to make new plants. Strawberry plants become less productive as they get older, so you should replace four-year-old plants. Strawberries are susceptible to many pests and diseases such as slugs, leaf blight, and mildew. To help prevent some of these, make sure you choose a more disease-resistant variety to start off with. Mulch around the plants with straw and make sure the plants have good airflow around them, and change their location every few years to prevent the build-up of disease. Keep a close eye on the plant, so you can act quickly if disease is detected.

To Harvest

Pick the strawberries when they are bright red and firm. You can use the young leaves and stems for tea, alongside the fresh fruit. Slice the fruit, leaving the stems on, and tear up some fresh leaves to enjoy a cup of fresh strawberry tea. To be able to have strawberry tea throughout the year, you need to dry the plant. Slice the fruit as

thinly as you can and place it on a flat sieve or flexible mesh screen. Keep it somewhere warm until dry. Your room will smell wonderful. If you dry the fruits in a dehydrator, they take about four to five hours to dry completely and will keep a lovely red color. To dry freshly picked leaves,

To Make Tea

pull them off their stems and wash well. Chop up the leaves and dry them in the air, a dehydrator, or an oven (see page 260). Store the fruits and the leaves separately in sealed glass containers in a dry and dark cupboard until needed.

Fill the kettle with fresh water. Bring the water to a boil, then pour some into your teacup or teapot to warm it up. Discard the water. Place four slices of strawberry fruit and a pinch of strawberry leaves and stems into a tea bag or teapot. Pour the boiled water (which should be between 176 to 185°F/80 to 85°C) over the tea and cover with a saucer or a lid. Allow the tea to steep for three minutes. Remove the tea bag or pour the tea from the teapot using a tea strainer and savor the delicious sweet strawberry taste. You can place a strawberry flower or one slice of fruit in the cup to serve. The tea has a beautiful pale pink color. On a really hot day, you can make strawberry sun tea. Put the fresh fruit and leaves into a mason jar or a jug and fill with cold water. Increase the quantity of fruit and leaves according to the size of your container; I use six strawberries, two leaves, and about 1 quart (1 liter) of water. Cover the jar or jug with a lid to stop insects from flying in. Place outside in direct sunlight for about five hours, depending on the sun's intensity. The warmth of the sun will bring out the flavor of the fruit. Strain through a jelly bag or fine-mesh sieve into a jug, and refrigerate until chilled. Serve with ice cubes that have strawberries frozen inside and a few strawberry flowers sprinkled on the top. This is an impressive and refreshing summer tea.

Tea Bag Friends

- Strawberries and mint have always been great partners. Prepare as before, adding a sprig of fresh mint leaves to the cup of strawberry tea. You can leave the mint leaves in the cup as you drink.

- Blend strawberry with hyssop for an antioxidant-boosting tea. Put two or three slices of strawberry, a small pinch of strawberry leaves, and a pinch of hyssop leaves into a tea bag or teapot and steep as before.

TIPS

Deer love strawberries, so protect your plants with netting if you need to.

Warning: Strawberries can cause an allergic reaction in some people.

FLOWERS

Calendula

Calendula officinalis

The Romans grew calendula for its medicinal qualities, and it is one of the oldest cultivated flowers. It belongs to the Asteraceae family and is commonly called pot marigold. It may have gained this name in Tudor times, when it was a popular ingredient in stews, soups, and pot-based cooking.

Calendula derives from the Latin word *kalendae*, meaning the day of the new moon or the start of the month in the Roman calendar. Calendula was believed to be able to flower at the start of any month of the year, hence its name. In its Latin name, *officinalis* denotes that the plant was recognized as an "official" and "useful" plant, which could be sold in an apothecary's shop. Calendula has bright yellow or orange, single or double flowers. Its long, hairy, aromatic leaves can also be used in tea.

Do not confuse calendula with French or African marigolds. They are both in the Asteraceae family, but marigolds are from the *Tagetes* genus, not *Calendula* genus. French and African marigolds are often recommended as a companion plant in your vegetable garden to keep pests away, but are not edible and so cannot be used for tea.

Medicinal Benefits

A powerful medicinal plant, calendula is known to be antiviral, antibacterial, and anti-inflammatory. It contains phosphorus and vitamin C and is good for gastrointestinal problems and to detoxify the digestive system. It may also help regulate women's hormones and can be used to help with premenstrual cramps. Gargling with cold calendula tea can soothe sore throats.

To Grow

Calendula should be grown as an annual and sown by seed each year. It is an easy plant to grow from seed and can be sown in seed trays in very early spring and kept inside until the warmer spring weather. Alternatively, it can be sown directly outside once the frosts have passed. It germinates very quickly, and the plant can be flowering within two months of sowing the seeds (see page 253). Calendula has amazing seeds that look a little like dried caterpillars. Children love studying them, and they are easy plants for children to grow.

Calendula need to be planted outside in a sunny place in well-drained soil. Space the plants 8 to 10 inches (20 to 25 cm) apart. They are well suited to growing in containers. Use a mixture of potting soil/compost and either grit or perlite, to help improve drainage. They do not like to dry out, so keep the soil moist, especially if you are growing them in a container. Strip off any

and combine the petals with the youngest, freshest leaves. Spread them out on a baking sheet or mesh screen and dry them in a low oven, turning them over every so often to ensure even drying. You can leave the flowers intact if you prefer to use the whole flower. The flowers heads take thirty to forty minutes to dry in the oven at 212°F (100°C). Turn the flower heads every ten minutes. They must be completely dry and crispy in order to be stored in a sealed glass container in a dry and dark cupboard.

old, dying leaves at the bottom of the plant throughout the season.

Cabbage moth and butterfly larvae can eat the leaves. Calendula can also be susceptible to powdery mildew; to prevent this, make sure your plants do not dry out and that they have enough ventilation. Calendula is great at self-seeding as long as a few flowers remain on the plant. Save your own seeds to sow in future years.

To Make Tea

Fill the kettle with fresh water. Bring the water to a boil, then pour some into your teacup or teapot to warm it up. Discard the

To Harvest

Harvest calendula flowers when in full bloom. Cut the remaining flower stems back to promote new flowers to grow. Use the fresh petals and leaves for one of the most beautiful-looking teas. To dry calendula, pick the petals off of the flowers

Tea Bag Friends

Try blending calendula with cilantro/coriander seeds for a light, fresh detox tea. Put a large pinch of calendula and two pinches of crushed cilantro seeds into a tea bag or teapot and infuse for three to four minutes. Remove the tea bag or pour the tea from the teapot using a tea strainer.

water. Put a pinch of dried or about four fresh leaves and a pinch of fresh or dried petals into a tea bag or teapot. Pour the boiled water (which should be between 176 to 185°F/80 to 85°C) over the tea. Allow the tea to steep for four minutes. Remove the tea bag or pour the tea from the tea pot using a tea strainer. You can serve with a couple of fresh calendula petals for decoration in the teacup. This is a gentle, slightly sweet tea. The leaves have a mild peppery but fresh green flavor. This is a lovely tea to drink on sunny afternoon.

TIPS

Spiritualists believed that calendula petals placed under your pillow would make your dreams come true!

Warning: Calendula should not be taken during pregnancy and some people may be allergic to calendula, so use with caution.

Chamomile

Chamaemelum nobile

Matricaria recutita

There are two main types of chamomile: Roman chamomile (*Chamaemelum nobile*) and German chamomile (*Matricaria recutita*). Both species can be used to make tea, but they have different life cycles and growing habits so choose the one suits your location the best. German chamomile is a taller plant and can grow to 2 feet (60 cm) tall. It is also known as manzanilla. Roman chamomile is a more compact, lower-growing perennial until it sends up tall flower stalks in the summer. It is also referred to as English chamomile and is often spelled "camomile" in the UK. Chamomile is native to Europe and North Africa where it is often found growing wild. It belongs to the Asteraceae family, the members of which have daisylike flowers. The flowers, stems, and leaves can be used to make wonderful tea. The name chamomile comes from the Greek word *khamaimelon*, which means "earth apple."

Medicinal Benefits

The flowers are antispasmodic and therefore can help with indigestion, stomach pain, upset stomachs, and painful gas. Chamomile can also help relax the body and is good for relieving anxiety and stress. It is a slight sedative, so it can help you get a good night's sleep. It is a great tea for calming children and can help with hay fever and boost your immune system.

To Grow

Growing Roman and German chamomile from seeds is the cheapest way to get lots of plants. Sow the seeds on a tray of seed-sowing compost/soil and cover with a very thin layer of soil—or better still, vermiculite—over the top (see page 250). Transplant the seedlings outside when they are large enough. You can sow the seeds straight into the garden after the frosts have finished in the spring. If you start with seedlings or small plants, transplant them into the garden or a container when the frosts have passed. Chamomile likes well-drained, sandy soil and ideally a position in full sun. Once it is established, it is a very hardy plant.

GERMAN CHAMOMILE
(Matricaria recutita)

German chamomile is sometimes known as wild chamomile and is the most commonly found species. It is an annual, which means it completes its life cycle in one year, so new plants need to be grown each year to continue your supply. However, it self-seeds easily, so allow some flowers to go to seed to propagate into new plants. It can grow up to 2 feet (60 cm) tall, so allow about 10 inches (25 cm) between each plant. It likes a sunny position and well-drained, sandy soil.

ROMAN CHAMOMILE
(Chamaemelum nobile)

This is a lovely neat, evergreen perennial, often grown into chamomile lawns. Choose your *Chamaemelum nobile* carefully, as some of the varieties grown specifically for lawns, such as *Chamaemelum nobile* "Treneague," do not produce flowers and so will not be suitable for tea. Roman chamomile spreads by its stems that creep outward and root when they find a suitable spot. You should trim the plants (keeping the clippings to use for tea) to encourage a dense bushy plant and remove any brown dead leaves throughout the year. In the spring, allow the plant to send up long stems on which flowers will develop.

You can buy *Chamaemelum nobile* "Flore Pleno," a very pretty double-flowered Roman chamomile variety that can also be used to make tea.

Both chamomiles are happy to be planted in a container. Fill your pot to the top with a mixture of grit and organic potting soil . The crown of the plant should be level with the soil. Both species flower from June to July. As well as sowing seeds, you can propagate new chamomile plants by dividing them in the spring (see page 251).

To Harvest

Chamomile blooms for a long time, so harvest throughout these months as and when the flowers are fully open. Cut the flowers off at the base of their stems to use for your tea. The stems and leaves also contain lots of wonderful flavor, so use these alongside the flowers. Chop them up into more manageable sizes and use fresh, or dry some to use at a later time. Dry on a flat sieve somewhere warm or in a dehydrator until completely crispy (see page 260). The leaves and stems will take a much shorter time to dry than the flowers. When com-

pletely dry, store in a sealed glass container in a dry, dark cupboard until needed.

To Make Tea

Fill the kettle with fresh water. Bring the water to a boil, then pour some into your teacup or teapot to warm it up. Discard the water. Put three or four flowers and a pinch of stems and leaves into a tea bag or teapot. The flowers are very strong and if too many are used, the tea can taste bitter. Pour the boiled water (which should be between 176 to 185°F/80 to 85°C) over the tea. Allow the tea to steep for three to five minutes. Remove the tea bag or pour the tea from the teapot using a tea strainer. There is a definite apple taste to the tea and it has a wonderful calming effect.

Tea Bag Friends

- Try blending chamomile with licorice for an immune-boosting and cleansing tea. Infuse a pinch of chamomile into a freshly made decoction of licorice root (page 243) and steep for three minutes. Strain into a teacup and drink.

- Try blending chamomile with mint for a digestive tonic. Put a small pinch of each into a tea bag or teapot and infuse for 3 minutes. Remove the tea bag or pour from the teapot using a tea strainer. Drink before or after a meal.

- Chamomile blended with lemon-scented pelargonium is a great calming tea to help with anxiety. Put a pinch of each in a teabag or teapot and infuse as before.

- To help with hayfever, try blending violets with chamomile. Put a pinch of each into a tea bag or teapot and infuse as before.

TIPS

- You can place cold chamomile tea bags on your eyelids to reduce puffiness.

- Chamomile is fairly pest- and disease-free, and in fact, it can help keep disease from other plants.

Warning: It is unusual, but people have been known to have an allergic reaction to chamomile, so as with all teas, use with caution. It is not recommended for use by pregnant women, as it can cause contractions.

Honeysuckle

Lonicera

oneysuckle is a highly scented climbing plant native to Europe, North Africa, North America, China, and India. The genus *Lonicera* was named after the German botanist Adam Lonicerus (Lonitzer), who in 1557, published *Kreuterbuch*, an important botanical reference book. The common name of honeysuckle was given for its sweet nectar, which is so delicious when sucked out of the flowers.

You can find evergreen or deciduous, climbing or low-growing, hardy or tender varieties of honeysuckle. The most common varieties are hardy climbers. All honeysuckle flowers can be harvested to make tea, and their fragrance can be incredible. *Lonicera periclymenum*, also called woodbine, is a common European honeysuckle. It is a tall-growing, deciduous, climbing plant, up to 20 feet (6 meters). *Lonicera* sempervirens (trumpet honeysuckle), a native of the eastern United States, can also grow up to 20 feet (6 meters) tall if left unpruned. It has long, orange, trumpet-shaped clusters of flowers and is loved by hummingbirds. *Lonicera japonica* (Japanese Honeysuckle) is native to Asia and has vanilla-scented white and yellow flowers. This is a vigorous plant, and its ability to spread and grow out of control in the wild has meant that this particular species is not allowed or encouraged in some states in the United States and in New Zealand. *Lonicera fragrantissima* is a low-growing type of honeysuckle with delicate white flowers that bloom in the winter and early spring. This species can be found growing wild in some US states. Most honeysuckle berries are poisonous so should not be eaten or used in tea.

Medicinal Benefits

Honeysuckle flowers have been valued for medicinal uses for hundreds of years. They are believed to help coughs and may help reduce a temperature. Honeysuckle can act as a laxative and diuretic, so it is used as a cleansing herb to help remove toxins from the body.

To Grow

It is easiest to start off with a plant, as seed germination is very slow. Choose a fragrant variety suitable to your location and follow the specific planting instructions. As a general rule, your honeysuckle would most like to be planted in a partly shaded place in your garden. It can be grown in a sunny position as long as it roots are kept cool and moist. Mulch around the honeysuckle with your own garden compost or well-rotted farmyard manure. This helps keep the roots moist and prevents powdery mildew from developing. Feed throughout the summer with an organic fertilizer.

Pruning for a lot of the varieties is done in the spring, but check your specific variety and prune as instructed on its label. You can take cuttings in the spring to grow more honeysuckle plants. Cut 2- to 3-inch (5 cm) long cuttings from non-flowering stems. If you need to grow your honeysuckle in a container, chose a low-growing, less vigorous variety. Do not allow the pot to dry out in the summer.

To Harvest

It is best to harvest the flowers when they first open, as the scent will be strongest then. Pick the petals off of the flowers. Do not use the leaves, as they make the tea bitter. Use the petals fresh or dry them for later use. They do not take long to dry, so choose a gentle method of drying such as on a mesh screen in a warm, well-ventilated room (see page 259). Once totally dry and crispy, store in a sealed glass container in a dry, dark cupboard until needed.

To Make Tea

Fill the kettle with fresh water. Bring the water to a boil, then pour some into your teacup or teapot to warm it up. Discard the water. Put about ten petals into a tea bag or teapot. Pour the boiled water (which should be between 176 to 185°F/80 to 85°C) over the tea. The petals will turn yellow when the hot water is poured on them. Allow the tea to steep for three minutes. Remove the tea bag or pour the tea from the teapot using a tea strainer. The tea is a pale yellow color and has a lovely mild floral taste with a calming effect. Try chilling this tea and serving it as an iced tea.

Tea Bag Friends

- Honeysuckle is delicious blended with ginger. Put a very small pinch of ginger and about ten honeysuckle petals into a tea bag or teapot. Infuse and serve as before.

- Try blending anise hyssop with honeysuckle for a soothing and warming tea. Put a pinch of each into a tea bag or teapot and infuse as before.

TIPS

Honeysuckle will attract lots of wildlife to your garden. I have a wonderful wood pigeon that sits and eats the shoots of mine in the wintertime.

Warning: Honeysuckle berries can be red, orange, or blue-black and most are poisonous. Do not eat them or use them for tea.

Jasmine

Jasminum sambac "Maid of Orleans"
and *Jasminum officinale*

asmine tea is one of the favorite teas in China, where it is known as *mo li hua cha*. It is made from the leaves of the *Camellia sinensis* plant (as an unoxidized green or oolong tea) suffused with the scent of *Jasminum sambac* flowers. The jasmine flowers are picked and laid alongside lightly steamed camellia leaves for a number of hours in a controlled environment. Overnight, the flowers open and release their scent, which then infuses into the camellia leaves. The process is repeated several times with batches of fresh jasmine flowers. This process is a great art and learned over generations. An even more complex and time-consuming process is to make a flowering jasmine tea. Flowers are sewn together with camellia leaves and made into flowering tea that unfurls like a blooming flower when brewed.

Jasminum sambac is sometimes referred to as Arabian jasmine, and its white flowers have an incredible perfume. You can get different varieties of *Jasminum sambac*, such as the single-flowered "Maid of Orleans," or the double-flowered "Grand Duke of Tuscany." *Jasminum sambac* is a tender plant, suitable to grow outside if you live in a warm tropical climate (USDA zone 9 or higher) or grown inside as a houseplant. It can be hard to grow and difficult and expensive to buy. An alternative is *Jasmine officinale*, or common jasmine, a deciduous climbing plant with fragrant white single flowers.

Medicinal Benefits

Drinking jasmine tea is supposed to reduce the heart rate, relieve sore muscles, and calm the whole body. It is believed to be an antidepressant and an aphrodisiac. It may even help slow the aging process and boost the immune system.

To Grow

Jasmines belong to the olive or Oleaceae family. This helps you to understand the conditions that the plants need to grow. To grow a sambac outside, you will need to live in a tropical climate. Your sambac will not tolerate a temperature lower than 50°F (10°C). You will need to grow your sambac inside if your climate does not allow. Sambacs need lots of light in order to flower—they ideally like 4 to 6 hours of sunshine a day—so place the plant in your sunniest windowsill. Pot it in a mix of perlite and organic potting soil for good drainage. Water it well but do not allow its roots to become soggy. If the leaves start to turn yellow, it has been overwatered. Feed the plant throughout the summer months with an organic fertilizer. You can take cuttings in the spring to create new plants (see page 251). Place your plant outside on warm days to enjoy some fresh air.

Jasmine officinale is a deciduous climbing plant with single white fragrant flowers. It can climb to great heights on a sheltered south-facing wall. It is still a tender plant, so would not withstand a harsh frost or temperatures below about 23°F (-5°C). Depending on your climate, it may need to be grown in a container and brought inside during the winter months. It can grow well in a conservatory or greenhouse. You can fit a trellis or a framework within the container for it to climb. Pot it in a mix of potting soil and perlite or grit for good drainage and water well in the summer. Feed your jasmine every month with an organic fertilizer during the summer growing season. You can prune it back after it has flowered to maintain a good shape and size. Cuttings can be taken in the late summer. You can buy cultivated varieties of *Jasmine officinale* with different-colored flowers and foliage.

To Harvest and Blend

Pluck the flowers from the stems. Use immediately for fresh jasmine flower tea or dry for jasmine green tea. Choose a more gentle method to dry your jasmine flowers, such as in the air in a warm, well-ventilated room. *J. sambac* flowers turn pink when they dry and over time will turn brown. You will need to blend the jasmine flowers with green tea leaves; follow the instructions on page 15 to make green tea. Place dried green tea leaves into a glass jar with some dried jasmine flowers. The more flowers there are, the stronger the jasmine flavor will be. Leave them in the sealed jar for a number of days—the longer the better—so that the jasmine fragrance can blend with the green tea. After at least a week it is ready to use.

To Make Tea

Fill the kettle with fresh water. Bring the water to a boil, then pour some into your teacup or teapot to warm it up. Discard the water. Put three infused green tea leaves and three or four jasmine flowers into a tea bag or teapot. Pour the boiled water

and then float a fresh jasmine flower in the tea to serve. Enjoy this amazing-tasting, homegrown blended tea.

To make a simple jasmine flower tea, put two pinches of fresh or dried jasmine flowers into a tea bag or teapot and steep as before. Place a fresh flower in the tea to serve.

Tea Bag Friends

- Jasmine's best friends are white and green tea.

- Blend with sweet tea vine for a possibly antiaging tea. Put two pinches of sweet tea vine and a pinch of jasmine flowers into a tea bag or teapot, cover, and steep as before.

TIPS

- Jasmine flowers are strung together into leis, or garlands, and are worn at weddings across Asia.

Warning: Carolina jasmine (*Gelsemium sempervirens*) or "false jasmine" is highly poisonous to humans. Make sure you use the full Latin name when buying your plants.

(which should be between 176 to 185°F/80 to 85°C) over the tea and cover with a saucer or a lid to trap the aroma. Allow the tea to steep for three minutes. Remove the tea bag or pour the tea using a tea strainer

Lavender

Lavandula angustifolia

avender is an aromatic herb with long, straight gray leaves and clusters of purple flowers on long stems. The name *Lavandula* is thought to have come from the Latin word *lavare*, which means to wash. To this day, we still like to use this fragrance in our washing products. It is a great plant to attract bees, butterflies, and insects to your garden, as the flowers are full of nectar for them to eat. There are hundreds of types of lavender, with a range of colors and sizes. Common or English lavender, *Lavandula angustifolia*, is best to use for making tea. There are many cultivars or types of *L. angustifolia*, so choose one that suits your location. I recommend *L. angustifolia* "Hidcote," which is low-growing, with silver-gray leaves and dark blue-purple flowers, or *L. angustifolia* "Munstead," which is a little taller and has gray-green leaves and lighter blue flowers. Both varieties are hardy, which means they should withstand temperatures below 5°F (-15°C).

Medicinal Benefits

Lavender is well known for its calming and relaxing qualities—therefore, drinking lavender tea will help with anxiety and stress. It is very good to drink before going to sleep as it helps with insomnia. It is also good at fighting cold and cough symptoms and easing stomach problems, and it is a natural antiseptic. It is good for the mind and body and helps promote overall well-being.

To Grow

You can grow lavender from seeds, but germination is difficult and the seeds may not turn out to be true to their parent plant. It is much easier to buy a plant so you can harvest its flowers for tea in the first year. It takes three years for a lavender plant to grow to full size.

Lavender can be grown in a container or directly in a garden in full sun and well-drained soil. Add some gravel or sharp sand if your soil is very heavy to improve drainage. Lavender prefers fairly alkaline soil (pH of 6.5 to 7), so add some organic compost and some garden lime if your soil is more acidic. Lavender does not like to have wet feet, so do not overwater. It is best to water it well and only water again when you notice it is dry. If you live in a region where temperatures drop to a very cold -20°F (-28°C), you should keep your lavender in a pot and bring it into a greenhouse to protect it from the frost, and then put it outside again the following spring.

It is very important to prune back your lavender plant every year; otherwise, it can become very woody and unattractive. In early spring, cut back the plant to about 2 inches (5 cm) above where the woody stems finish (it will not regrow if you cut into the woody stems). New green stems will develop from there.

You can take hardwood cuttings from lavender after the plant has flowered in late summer.

To Harvest

You can pick fresh lavender flowers and leaves as and when you need them for a cup of fresh lavender tea. It is ideal to pick the flowers before they fully open. Cut long stems of lavender and tie small bunches together with a rubber band. Hang the bunches somewhere cool and dark, with good ventilation to prevent any mold from developing. Keep an eye on the flowers, as the length of time it should hang for will vary. When you can feel the heads are crispy, dry, and brittle, it is ready to be taken down. Break off the flower heads and store them in a sealed glass container in the dark until needed. If you are only drying a few flowers at a time, put them in a flat sieve or on a baking sheet and leave them somewhere warm for three to four days until the heads are completely dry. Store in a sealed glass container somewhere dry and dark until needed.

To Make Tea

Fill the kettle with fresh water. Bring the water to a boil, then pour some into your teacup or teapot to warm it up. Discard the water. Put two or three heads of lavender and a few leaves into a tea bag or teapot. Pour the boiled water (which should be between 176 to 185°F/80 to 85°C) over the tea and cover with a saucer or a lid. Allow the tea to steep for three minutes, then remove the tea bag or pour the tea from the teapot using a tea strainer, and enjoy. Lavender makes a strong and fragrant floral tea. To use dried lavender, put a pinch or a teaspoon of dried lavender flowers and leaves into a tea bag or teapot and steep for three to four minutes. Drink, relax, and fall asleep!

Tea Bag Friends

- You can blend lavender flowers with green or black tea. Put some dried flower heads into a jar with some dried green or black tea leaves, and let sit for a few weeks to allow the flavors to blend together.

- Lavender is also very good blended with bergamot. Put a small pinch of lavender and a pinch of bergamot into a tea bag and steep as before. This is a very good tea to help with stress and depression.

- Blend with sweet tea vine for an overall-good-health tea. Put a pinch of lavender flowers and a pinch of sweet tea vine leaves into a tea bag or teapot, cover, and steep as before.

TIPS

Lavender can be used as a flavor in many baking recipes. And if you needed another reason to grow it, deer and rabbits and slugs tend to dislike the taste, so it's fairly pest-proof.

Rose

Rosa

There are many different species and cultivated varieties of fragrant roses. Tea roses and hybrid tea roses are named as such because their fragrance was supposed to be similar to Chinese tea. You do not have to choose a "tea rose" to make tea—choose a color and size of highly fragrant rose to suit your location.

Medicinal Benefits

Rose petal tea is thought to help cleanse the bladder and kidneys and prevent digestive problems. It is also used to help with stress and can calm the nervous system. As with all teas, drink in moderation, as rose petals can be a laxative and may cause diarrhea if taken in excess.

To Grow

If you want to make rose bud tea, hybrid musk varieties, such as "Ballerina," "Felicia," and "Prosperity" are recommended, as they produce small fragrant buds. If you would like to harvest petals rather than buds, you can choose any very fragrant rose of any size and color. Recommendations of hybrid tea varieties include "Scentsation," "Fragrant Cloud," or "Renaissance." You can get beautiful climbing and rambling fragrant roses but these may take a couple of years to reward you with flowers. Shrub roses are a good starting point if you are new to growing roses, as these can be very fragrant, easy to grow, disease resistant, and require little, if any pruning. Most roses like a sunny position, but check the preferences of your specific variety.

If you are planting your roses in the garden, first stand your plant in a bucket of water for ten minutes to completely soak the roots. Dig a hole that is much larger than the pot or root size to give the roots room to grow. Mix some fertilizer such as bonemeal into the soil that will be going back into the hole. Remove the plant from the pot, loosen the roots, and set it in the hole, making sure that the base of the stems is not below the soil level. Fill the soil around the roots, compacting the ground with your boot.

You can grow roses in containers as long as you choose a suitable variety. Make sure you never let your roses dry out. Feed your roses an organic fertilizer once a month from spring until the end of the growing season in late summer for really strong plants. Some roses require pruning in the early spring, so check your plant label for specific pruning advice.

To Harvest

The great thing about growing your own roses is that you know that the flowers will be free of any chemical sprays. It's hard to do, but you should harvest the rose petals when the flowers are looking their best as they will have the most aroma at that time. Some large rose petals have a white part at the base of the petal. These can be bitter, so remove if necessary. Use secateurs or scissors to cut off the rose buds once they

have opened a little. In order to store your roses, you need to dry them. The petals can be dried on a flat sieve or a baking sheet set in a warm spot. The rose buds will need to be dried in a low oven or in a dehydrator. If you are drying buds and petals together, keep checking them and remove the petals sooner, as the petals will take a much shorter time to dry than the buds. It is important that all the moisture is removed from the buds or they will go moldy when they are stored.

To Make Tea

Fill the kettle with fresh water. Bring the water to a boil, then pour some into your teacup or teapot to warm it up. Discard the water. Put four pinches of rose petals or five rose buds into a tea bag or teapot. This amount will vary according to your taste, so experiment. Pour the boiled water (which should be between 176 to 185°F/80 to 85°C) over the tea and cover with a saucer or a lid to trap the beautiful aroma. Allow the tea to steep for three to five minutes. Remove the tea bag or pour the tea from the teapot using a tea strainer, and enjoy. The color of the tea will be determined by the color of the rose petals. Whatever the color, the peppery taste and fragrant aroma of this tea are divine.

Tea Bag Friends

- Roses are wonderful mixed with black tea. It is a great idea to mix up a jar of this tea in advance to give the roses time to infuse with the black tea. This can make a wonderful gift, too.

- Chicory blended with rose petal is a great cleansing tea. Put a pinch of rose petals into a freshly made chicory decoction and steep for three minutes (see Chicory, page 227). Strain to serve.

TIPS

Bunches of roses from shops are not suitable to use for tea, as they may have been sprayed with chemicals.

Saffron

Crocus sativus

Saffron is the bright red stigma and style on the flower of the *Crocus sativus* plant. It is the most expensive spice in the world. Each flower produces only three stigmas that have to be picked by hand, so harvesting is incredibly labor intensive. It is now grown commercially all over the world including Iran, India, Morocco, and Europe (particularly in Spain). This crocus only flowers for a few weeks each fall. The fragrant flowers are a lovely pale mauve color and the plant has thin, swordlike, dark green leaves. Crocuses grow from a corm, not a bulb. Corms and bulbs are underground food storage organs. A corm is the swollen and condensed underground stem of the plant, unlike a bulb, which is a condensed shoot surrounded by layers of modified leaves. The saffron corms take two years to become mature enough to produce flowers. Each subsequent year, numerous new corms will replace the main corm. Some crocuses are toxic so it is vital to use the Latin name and make sure you buy *Crocus sativus*.

Medicinal Benefits

Saffron tea has a warm, happy, feel-good effect and can help with many health issues. Known as the flower of health, saffron is a powerful antioxidant and antiseptic. It may help with the buildup of gas and aids digestion. It is also thought to be good for the heart and mind and can treat depression. There are reports that it helps the body fight cancer.

To Grow

Crocus sativus need a sunny and sheltered spot, ideally with neutral or slightly alkaline soil. If you start with fifty mature corms, you should grow enough saffron to make quite a few cups of saffron tea. Try and buy the largest corms you can (1 inch or larger) as this will mean they are a few years old, so you will get flowers in your first year. It is best to plant the corms in the summer when they do not have leaves, as it gives them time to settle in before they flower. If planting in your garden, mix in some fertile organic homemade compost from your composter or horse manure into the ground. Plant the corms with the shoot pointing upward about 6 inches (15 cm) apart and about 6 inches (15 cm) deep—much deeper than you imagine. Planting

them this far apart gives the corms room to grow and the depth promotes flowering. It also protects them from being dug up by squirrels and other animals.

It is best not to buy saffron while it is still in leaf, as this is when it is making its food for the following year, and moving it around will disturb this process. However, if you do buy saffron corms while they have their leaves on, plant them in pots as soon as you have received them. Water and feed them until the leaves die back in the spring. Then transplant the corms from the pot into the ground (as above) in the

may be overcrowded and need separating to allow them more room; otherwise, they will stop flowering. In early summer, dig up the corms, separate them, and plant them individually and in a new location to help prevent disease. You can grow saffron in a container outside as long as it is deep enough (at least 12 inches/30 cm).

To Harvest

For the best saffron, harvest when the flowers are in bud and not fully open. Using tweezers, carefully pluck the long dark red stigmas from the flower center. Dry the stigmas by layering them between paper towels and placing them somewhere dry with constant warmth, such as an airing cupboard. Keep an eye on them, as they will not take long to dry. When a stigma crackles, it is completely dry and ready to be stored in an airtight container in a dark place. The color of the saffron will darken over time, and if stored correctly, it can last for up to five years.

early summer. They flower for about three weeks in the fall when the weather gets colder. Each flower will only last for about a day so it is important not to miss the precious harvest.

The flowers are sterile and do not make seeds; the corms are the plant's method of reproduction. After four years, the corms

To Make Tea

Fill the kettle with fresh water. Bring the water to a boil, then pour some into your teacup or teapot to warm it up. Discard the water. Put a pinch (10 to 15 strands) of fresh or dried saffron into a tea bag or teapot. Pour the boiled water (which should be between 176 to 185°F/80 to 85°C) over the tea. Allow the tea to steep for three minutes. The water will quickly turn a deep yellow color. Remove the tea bag, or pour the tea from the teapot using a tea strainer. The tea has a bittersweet, hay-like taste, and it gives a relaxing and heart-warming sensation. Reuse the saffron for 2 or more infusions.

TIPS

DO NOT confuse true saffron with safflower (*Carthamus tinctorius*), commonly called American or Portuguese saffron. This flower is used for the bright yellow dyelike color it imparts, but it is a completely different plant and will be very cheap to buy in comparison to real saffron.

Tea Bag Friends

- Saffron is amazing with rosemary for a feel-good tea. Put a pinch of rosemary and four or five strands of saffron into a tea bag or teapot and infuse as before. This tea has a strong flavor and a strong yellow color.

- Blend manuka with saffron for a good-health tea. Put a pinch of manuka and a few strands of saffron into a tea bag or teapot, cover, and infuse as before. Enjoy the flavorsome, aromatic tea.

- Cardamom is wonderful blended with saffron, as the saffron gives this otherwise clear tea a yellow color. Put a small pinch of cardamom and a large pinch of saffron into a tea bag or teapot and infuse as before. This is a great pick-me-up tea to help lift your mood and combat stress.

Violet

Viola odorata

Violets belong to the *Viola* genus in the Violaceae family. They are native to Asia and Europe and are now widely cultivated garden plants. *Viola odorata* are low-growing, evergreen perennials and are commonly known as sweet violet, English violet, or wood violet. Their delicately perfumed flowers are one of the first flowers to appear in the spring, and they really are a hidden delight to have in your garden.

There are many cultivated varieties of *Viola odorata* to choose from, with purple, pink, or white single flowers. To make the best tea, choose a highly scented variety that flowers prolifically. Violets are thought to bring good fortune and are a symbol of good luck. They were Napoleon's favorite flower, and were worn by his wife, Josephine, on her wedding day. During Victorian times, the violet triumphed in popularity, being used for tea and many other culinary dishes. Another species of viola, *Viola tricolor* or wild pansy, is known as "Heartease" because of its heart-shaped leaves. This species can also be used to make tea.

Medicinal Benefits

Violet flowers and leaves can be used to make tea. Violets are anti-inflammatory, antiseptic, and antifungal. The leaves contain a lot of vitamin C and may help with hayfever and sinus congestion. They may also help relieve headaches and reduce anxiety. It can have a laxative effect and should not be taken in excess.

To Grow

Violets can be difficult and time consuming to grow from seed because they need a cold period to germinate. Sow seeds in the winter and leave in a cold greenhouse until new shoots appear in the spring. Mice and ants like to eat violet seeds, so cover the tray with a sheet of glass or a plastic bag to help protect them until they germinate. It is easier to start off with some small plug plants or starters. Transplant these into a mix of organic potting soil and grit to improve drainage. Re-pot the plant as it grows and feed your violet every spring.

You can plant your violet in the ground. They particularly like to be planted beneath deciduous trees or shrubs so that they experience summer shade and winter sunshine.

Seed-producing flowers grow in the late summer/fall, so if you do not want seeds spread all over your garden, remove these before they are ripe. Seeds are ripe

when they are brown inside the seedpod. Violets also reproduce by making runners. Take the runner off and if it has a small root developing, pot it and make a new plant. Removing the runners also encourages the plant to make more flowers. Mulching the plants with organic homemade compost helps to feed the violets and keeps them moist, too. *Viola odorata* do not like heat, so they are not suitable to be grown inside. If you only have inside space, such as a windowsill, you can choose to grow Parma violets, which are tender and not frost resistant (USDA Zone 8). They have double flowers and a different perfume and taste.

To Harvest

Harvest the flowers you have grown yourself to be sure there are no chemical sprays on them. They flower from early spring, so harvest once the flowers are in full bloom, as this is when they have the most scent. Nip off the flowers and leaves at the base on the stem, leaving enough leaves for the plant to continue to grow happily. Then remove the stems from the harvested flowers and leaves and they are ready to be used in a cup of fresh violet tea. Dry the flowers and leaves to store for later use (see page 259). They do not take a long time to dry and the flowers will keep their beautiful color.

quart (1 liter) of water. Pour on boiled water and allow to infuse for 5 minutes. Strain the liquid through a sieve into a bowl or jug and leave to cool at room temperature. Cover and refrigerate for a few hours until well chilled. Serve with violets frozen in ice cubes.

To Make Tea

Fill the kettle with fresh water. Bring the water to a boil, then pour some into your teacup or teapot to warm it up. Discard the water. Put six flowers and four leaves into a tea bag or teapot (add more if you prefer a stronger flavor). Pour the boiled water (which should be between 176 to 185°F/80 to 85°C) over the tea. Allow the tea to steep for three minutes. If you have used purple flowers your tea will be turning a beautiful blue color. Remove the tea bag or pour the tea from the teapot using a tea strainer. Put one fresh flower in the cup as decoration, and enjoy. Violet tea has a very mild, gentle taste and a sweet violet flavor and aroma.

To make violet iced tea, make the tea in the same way but use larger amounts of violets according to the size of your jug or container. I use two handfuls of violet flowers, one handful of leaves, and about 1

- Violet tea is very mild tasting, so serve it with a slice of fresh lemon.

- To help with hayfever, try blending violets with chamomile. Put a pinch of each into a tea bag or teapot and infuse as before.

- For a tea to help with sinus discomfort you can try a decoction of myrtle infused with a tea bag of violet. Steep the violet for 3 minutes in the strained myrtle decoction (see myrtle, page 156). Remove the tea bag to serve.

- Violet is also good to blend with black tea. Make up a bag of dried violets and black tea and set aside to allow the flavors to infuse. Steep and serve as you would regular black tea, without milk.

TIPS

DO NOT confuse African violets with violets. They are a completely different plant and are not edible. It is vital to clearly identify a plant before using it.

ROOTS

Angelica

Angelica archangelica

Angelica is a biennial plant, and some species can grow up to 5 feet (1½ meters) tall. It has large ornamental stems and serrated light green leaves. There are many varieties of *Angelica*, but *archangelica* is the main one used for medicinal purposes. It is a plant that has been revered for its medicinal use for over a thousand years. There are two folk tales about how it was named. An angel was said to have appeared to a monk, holding the plant, saying that it could cure the plague. It was also believed to be named angelica as it flowers on the feast day of the archangel Michael. The root is the most medicinal part of the plant, but you can also use young leaves and stems to make angelica tea. In China a species of angelica called "Dong Quai," or *Angelica sinensis*, is used and known as "female ginseng."

Medicinal Benefits

Angelica tea is excellent for all-around good health. It contains vitamin B12, folic acid, and niacin. It increases bloodflow and can help with headaches, and is good for people with high blood pressure. It is a warming herb and can improve circulation. It helps with digestion and can relieve stomach pain, flatulence, colic, and indigestion.

To Grow

It is easiest to buy a plant in the very early spring to start off. Angelica can be planted in any type of soil, preferably in a partly shaded spot. It loves moist soil, so it would be well suited to an area near a pond or marsh. If you do not have a garden it can be planted into a larger pot and placed on a balcony. Keep it well watered and remove any dead yellow leaves. If it is allowed to go to seed in its second year, collect the seeds from the flower head in late summer and sow them while they are still ripe (within three weeks). Sow the seeds in a seed tray without covering them with soil, and place the tray on a windowsill or in a greenhouse. When the seedlings are about 0.7 inch (2 cm) tall, separate them and transplant into pots. Grow these inside un-

til the following spring when you will have fresh new angelica plants to grow outside. They can self-seed if planted in a garden.

To Harvest

Harvest the leaves and stems in the summer when they are young and fresh. Chop

them up into small pieces and use fresh, or dry them for later use alongside the root. Harvest the root in the autumn of its first or second year before it dies back. Dig up the plant or remove it from the pot and clean off the soil. Break off the smaller roots to leave the main root system. Wash as much of the soil off as you can. Chop the roots into very small pieces and put them in a sieve. Wash very well under cold water, picking out any lumps of soil or stones. When the root is completely clean, spread it out on a tray and dry in an oven or in a dehydrator. When it is completely hard and dry, it is ready to use. The root should not be used fresh.

To Make Tea

You need to make a decoction of dried angelica root rather than a simple infusion. The harder root needs to be heated for a longer time before it releases its medicinal properties. Place a small pinch of dried root and 1½ cups of water in a small saucepan, cover, and simmer for ten to fifteen minutes. Strain the liquor through a tea strainer into a teacup. Serve hot.

To use the leaves and stem with the

root, place a pinch of dried or fresh leaves into a tea bag. Put the tea bag into a cup of hot freshly made, strained root liquor for three minutes then remove the bag. This is a strong tea with an acquired, slightly soapy taste. It has a slight numbing effect on the mouth and a calming effect on the body.

Tea Bag Friends

- The flavor of angelica is improved by blending it with lemon balm. Add a pinch of lemon balm to your angelica leaf tea bag and steep in the freshly made root liquor as before.

- Try blending angelica with cilantro/coriander seeds. Add a pinch of angelica root to a pinch of crushed cilantro seeds to a small saucepan and brew a decoction as before. A great digestive tea.

TIPS

Angelica atropurpurea, or American angelica, can be found growing wild in North America. It has lovely architectural purple stems and can reach over 6 feet (2 meters) tall. Do not use this species to make tea, as its root has a very bitter, unpleasant taste.

Warning: Angelica should not be used by pregnant or breast-feeding women or diabetics. This tea can have adverse affects and can cause nausea in some people. Use with caution

Chicory

Cichorium intybus

Chichorium intybus has long stems with beautiful blue flowers that open during the day. It is often found growing wild in Europe and America and is commonly called blue dandelion. It is grown for its root from which a highly medicinal tea can be made. It can also be roasted and used as a caffeine-free coffee substitute. There are many other different types of chicory that have been cultivated. Most people will know it as a vegetable that looks similar to a lettuce or cabbage. The species *Chichorium intybus* includes "Whitloof" (Belgian chicory), "Red Verona" (red chicory), and "Pain de Sucre" (Sugar Loaf) chicory. These varieties are grown for their leaves and used in winter salads. It is the common *Chichorium intybus* which you need to make tea. You can also use chicory flowers and young leaves to add to the root for tea.

Medicinal Benefits

Chicory is high in protein and is rich in vitamins A, C, B, and K. There are many medical claims for chicory including that it can alleviate premenstrual symptoms, help to lower cholesterol, and aid weight loss. It is believed to help the body absorb calcium and eliminate toxins in your blood and liver. Many people have a cup of chicory tea before a meal to help with digestion.

To Grow

Chicory is a hardy perennial, which means it lives for more than one year. Every year the roots will expand into a larger more established network and every winter after it has flowered, it dies back, and will come up again the following spring.

You can grow chicory from seeds in the spring from April to May. Sow seeds thinly as instructed on the seed packet, into a tray or small pots, and place on a sunny windowsill or in a warm greenhouse. Keep watered. When the seedlings are about ¼ inch (2 cm) tall, separate them. Lift and replant the seedlings into small pots and grow them inside until you have a small plant.

In order to harvest chicory in your first year, buy a two- or three-year-old plant in the springtime. Plant it in the garden in a sunny place, bearing in mind that each plant will grow to around 3 feet (90 cm) tall. If you want to grow chicory in a pot or container, choose a very deep pot (about 24 inches/60 cm deep), as the taproot needs room to grow.

To Harvest

Dig up the plant in the late autumn before the ground freezes. Be careful to lift the whole root, so loosen the soil around the plant before pulling it out. If you would like to keep some of the plant to grow for next year, divide the root where you can see a new shoot developing. Plant this back into a pot or in the ground. Take the root you want to use and cut off the top of the plant. The root is very hard so use

a serrated knife to cut either side of the root and then snap it off with your hands. Wash the root using a scrubbing brush to remove any remaining soil. Pick some of the beautiful flowers and leaves to use alongside the root. Peel the root and then slice it into pieces. You will find the top of the root too hard to slice, but remove

as much as you can. It is now ready to use fresh or can be dried for later use. To dry the root, spread it on a baking sheet and place it in a low oven (212°F/100°C or lower). Break the slices into smaller pieces when they are completely dry. To dry the flowers and leaves spread them out on a tray or flat sieve and leave in a warm room or near a radiator, turning them every so often. When they are totally dry and crispy they can be stored. Place the leaves and flowers and root in separate sealed glass containers and keep in a dry dark cupboard until needed.

To Make Tea

You need to make a decoction of chicory root. The harder root needs to be heated for a longer time to release its medicinal properties and flavor. Place a small pinch of dried root and 1½ cups of water in a small saucepan, cover, and simmer for ten to fifteen minutes. Strain the liquid through a tea strainer into a teacup. Serve hot. You can add a pinch of dried leaves and flowers to the freshly made root decoction. Infuse for three minutes. Strain and serve. For a beautiful tea, drop a fresh chicory flower head into the teacup before drinking. This tea does not have an aroma but it tastes sweet, and a little like fudge!

Echinacea

Echinacea

chinacea is an attractive herbaceous perennial that is easy to grow in most gardens. It is also known as coneflower or purple coneflower. Native Americans have used echinacea as a medicinal plant for hundreds of years. The name comes from the Greek word *echinos*, meaning "hedgehog," because of its prickly central flower cone. It can be found growing wild in many US states, but it is now protected in its native habitat and must not be picked.

There are three species of echinacea used for medicinal purposes, all of which are suitable to use for tea: *Echinacea purpurea*, *Echinacea augustifolia*, and *Echinacea pallida*. *E. purpurea* has a sweet scented flower with less drooping petals than *E. augustifolia*. *E. pallida* (illustrated in the painting), has thin drooping petals that are a light pink color, and thin pointed leaves. You can add an infusion of the leaves and flowers to the root.

Medicinal Benefits

Echinacea is an herb that is still commonly used by many people. It is widely believed that it strengthens the immune system to fight sore throats, colds, and flu. It may be most effective if taken at the early stages of infection. It may also help with digestion.

To Grow

Echinacea is a lovely plant to have at the back of a flowerbed or in pots to give some height and color to your garden throughout the summer. An echinacea plant must

be at least three years old before you can harvest it's root for tea, so buy a mature plant to begin with. More plants can easily be grown in the spring from seed, and these can be harvested in future years. Echinacea likes well-drained, fertile soil and a sunny position. Prepare your soil by mixing in some homemade compost or well-rotted manure. If you are growing in a pot, mix 50 percent potting soil with 50 percent perlite or fine grit to help improve the drainage. You can mulch around your more established plants with manure in the springtime or use a liquid seaweed fertilizer throughout the summer if you are growing them in a pot. Once established, you can divide your echinacea plants in the fall when they have died back. Split the roots apart using a fork or spade and replant or pot as before. Allow some flowers to go to seed and save some seeds to sow the following year.

To Harvest

In the fall when the leaves have died back, dig up your plant. Cut off a portion of root, leaving enough so that you can replant the echinacea and it can continue to grow. Wash the root you are harvesting, using a scrubbing brush to get rid of any dirt. Chop the clean root into small pieces and dry them (see page 259). You can also use the flowers and leaves of the echinacea plant. Harvest the flowers and leaves any time from June/July throughout the summer. The flowers should be picked just before they fully open. Chop up the leaves and flowers and dry them and spread them out on a baking tray or fine-mesh sieve and place somewhere warm and dry, turning them every so often. When the plant is completely dry and crispy store in a sealed glass container in a dry, dark cupboard until needed. Dry the roots in the same way or in a low oven (see page 259). Store the dried roots in a separate container.

To Make Tea

To make a decoction of echinacea, place two pinches of echinacea root and 1½ cups of water in a small saucepan, cover, and bring to a boil. Then reduce the heat and simmer for ten to fifteen minutes. The liquid will have a strong yellow color. Add a pinch of echinacea leaves and flowers to the freshly made decoction and steep for three minutes. Strain into a teacup to serve. The leaves and flowers turn the tea an olive green color. Enjoy this calming and relaxing tea. It has an earthy taste and gives a tingling sensation on the tongue.

- Blend echinacea with a pinch of lemon or orange thyme for a cold- and cough-fighting tea. Put a pinch of thyme into a freshly made echinacea decoction and steep for three minutes. Strain into a teacup to drink.

- I find the taste of echinacea improves when blended with lavender as this also gives the tea an aroma. Put a pinch of lavender into a freshly made echinacea decoction, cover and steep for three minutes. Strain into a teacup to drink.

- For a digestion-boosting tea, serve an echinacea decoction with a slice of fresh ginger.

TIPS

The flowers have strong upright stems that make them perfect to use in flower arrangements.

Warning: Some people are allergic to echinacea. If you are at all concerned, consult a medical practitioner before using echinacea. You should consume this tea in moderation.

Ginger

Zingiber officinale

Ginger is an ancient plant that was introduced to the New World more than a thousand years ago from Asia. It is grown for its rhizome, or swollen underground stem, which is why it is often called stem ginger. (I have listed it in the "root" section of this book for simpler categorization.) It belongs to the Zingiberaceae family, which includes cardamom and turmeric. *Zingiber officinale* is reluctant to flower and has insignificant blooms, but this is the species you need to grow to harvest for tea. Other species of ginger have amazing flowers. *Zingiber officinale* has long, pointed, almost bamboolike green leaves. Ginger is now commercially grown in Asia, Africa, South America, the Caribbean, and Australia. In the Philippines, a decoction of ginger is called Salabat tea.

Medicinal Benefits

Ginger tea is good for digestion and may help with nausea and travel sickness. Essential oils found in ginger are antibacterial, so it is very good to take regularly for overall well-being. It is believed to help relieve muscle strain after exercise and is used to help ease the pain of arthritis. It is a popular winter drink and is used to boost the body's defenses against colds and flu. As with all teas, consume in moderation, especially if you are pregnant.

To Grow

Ginger needs to be grown as a houseplant unless you live in a tropical climate with a minimum temperature of 86°F (30°C). Buy an established plant to start off, as this means you should be able to harvest fresh ginger in your first year. The more mature the rhizome, the stronger the taste will be. Keep the plant well watered, but not over-watered, and mist the leaves with water every so often. If the leaves develop brown tips, the plant may not be getting enough water. Feed with an organic fertilizer such as liquid seaweed every few weeks during the summer growing season, as gingers are hungry plants. In the fall, when the light levels are decreasing in a temperate climate,

slowly stop watering the plant to encourage the leaves to die down. By winter, the leaves should have all died off, but this does not mean the plant is dead. Pull off the dry brown leaves so that only the rhizome remains. Your ginger is now dormant and no growth is taking place. Do not water it. Store it somewhere cool and dry. If you don't want what appears to be an empty pot in your house over the winter you can remove the rhizome from the soil and store it in a cool, dry place until spring. Re-pot your ginger when the weather warms, and water it regularly again. Buds will develop into new leaves and the plant will reawaken.

You can grow fresh ginger from a rhizome purchased at the grocery store. Choose a plump and firm-looking rhizome with buds already formed. Fill a pot with a mixture of 50 percent potting soil and 50 percent vermiculite or perlite, to help with

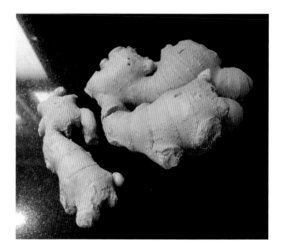

drainage. Plant the ginger so that the bud is just below the surface of the soil and is pointing upward. Water the ginger and then cover the pot with a plastic bag secured with a rubber band. When you can see the bud growing, remove the bag. It may take a few years to grow a ginger large enough to harvest, but this is a cheap way of obtaining your own ginger plant. If you live in a tropical climate, it is easy to grow ginger in the ground or in a pot outside. In this instance, it likes fertile, well-drained soil, and a semi-sunny position with lots of water. Mulch the ground to help with water loss and feed the plant every few weeks.

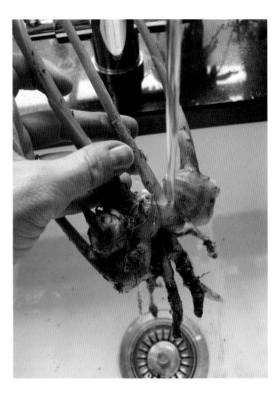

To Harvest

Your ginger will have achieved its maximum yearly growth by the fall, so harvest it at any point around this time, as long as it is established enough. If your rhizome is big enough, you can split it and replant some for next year. You can increase the amount you harvest each year as your plant develops. Wash off the selected roots and rhizomes using a brush and make sure all of the soil is removed. You will see more clearly the roots and the rhizomes at this point. Cut off the top stems and the big and small roots to leave just the rhizomes. Grate these and use fresh or spread on a flat

sieve or mesh screen and leave somewhere warm to dry or spread out on a tray in low temperature oven (see page 259). When totally dry and hard, store in a sealed glass container in a dry, dark cupboard until needed.

To Make Tea

Homegrown ginger is wonderfully fresh and juicy in comparison to the drier and more fibrous store-bought ginger. A cup of freshly grated ginger tea has a gentle warming sensation so it is a great winter

aroma. Allow the tea to steep for three minutes, then remove the tea bag or pour the tea from the teapot using a tea strainer and enjoy. It has an amazing spicy lemony flavor. It is also great as an iced tea. Brew as before, allow to cool, and then refrigerate until well chilled. Serve with ice cubes and a slice of fresh ginger.

tea. Fill the kettle with fresh water. Bring the water to a boil, then pour some into your teacup or teapot to warm it up. Discard the water. Put two pinches of fresh or dried ginger into a tea bag or teapot. Pour the boiled water (which should be between 176 to 185°F/80 to 85°C) over the tea and cover with a saucer or a lid to contain the

Tea Bag Friends

- Blend ginger with sweet tea vine for a body-balancing tea. Put a pinch of sweet tea vine with a pinch of ginger into a tea bag or teapot and steep as before. This may be a good tea to help recovery after overexertion.

- Try blending licorice with ginger for a cold- and flu-defense tea. Make a decoction (see Licorice, page 246) using a pinch of ginger and a pinch of licorice root in the saucepan. This is a strong-tasting tea with a real zing to it.

- Honeysuckle is delicious blended with ginger. Put a very small pinch of ginger and a large pinch (about ten petals) of honeysuckle flowers into a tea bag or teapot and infuse as before.

TIPS

Fresh ginger can be made into crystallized ginger for a sweet treat. Cut up a fresh ginger rhizome into slices. Combine 1 cup of ginger, 1 cup of water, and 1 cup of sugar in a saucepan and simmer for fifteen to twenty minutes. Strain the ginger (be sure to save the syrup to use over ice cream or another dessert) and then coat the slices in more sugar. Leave to cool and then eat.

Licorice
Glycyrrhiza glabra

icorice (spelled liquorice in the UK and Australia) is from the Leguminosae or pea family. It is an herbaceous perennial so it will die down in the colder winter months. It has small light blue to purple flowers and wonderful long seedpods, but you may not see these unless you live in a warm climate. It has pointed, oval-shaped, green leaves that grow in pairs along the stems. It is native to southern Europe, Asia, and northern Africa.

Licorice has been taken medicinally for thousands of years. The Greeks used it to treat asthma and Alexander the Great gave it to his troops to chew on long marches, to quench their thirst and improve their endurance. The name *Glycyrrhiza* comes from the Greek words *glukos*, meaning sweet, and *riza*, meaning root. It contains a compound called glycyrrhizin that is fifty times sweeter than sugar, hence why this plant is sometimes called sweet root.

Medicinal Benefits

There are believed to be so many medicinal benefits of licorice that it is hard to know where to begin. Licorice is an anti-inflammatory and may help with stomach, urinary, and intestinal problems, as well as heartburn and acid reflux. It is good for mouth and stomach ulcers, and helps reduce the pain of sore throats, which is why it is often made into lozenges. It is believed to help clean the liver by removing toxins from the body, and it may help lower cholesterol. It may also help to reduce stress and relieve depression.

To Grow

You can sow licorice seeds in the early spring, but germination can be erratic. Pot seedlings when they are about ½ inch (2 cm) tall and keep them inside to protect them from late frosts. The seedlings can be planted outside when the weather is warm. Try to buy a more developed plant (two to three years old) to start off, as the roots take a few years to grow large enough to harvest. Plant it in well-drained, rich, sandy soil in a sunny position. As with peas, the licorice roots actually fix nitrogen in the soil so the ground actually benefits from having licorice planted in it. It is quite an unruly plant so cut back leggy stems to encourage new growth from the bottom. You can grow it in a container if you have no alternative and especially while the plant is young. Licorice is hardy once the plant is established, so bring it into an unheated greenhouse or windowsill during colder months if it is less than two years old.

You can propagate the plant by splitting the established root in the fall. Find a long piece of root that has a bud on it, and separate it. Plant in a pot with a mix of 60 percent organic potting compost and 40 percent sharp sand or horticultural grit. Harvest part of the root at this time. Your plant will die back over the winter and all the foliage will disappear. You hardly need to water it at this time. In the spring, new shoots will appear.

To Harvest

Each year, you should be able to harvest a larger amount of licorice. Once you have dug it up, wash the roots under cold running water, using a scrubbing brush to get in between the smaller roots. Using scissors, cut up the thinner pieces of roots into small pieces. Use a knife to cut the larger part of the root into thin slices.

To dry licorice, place the root on a baking sheet in the oven at a low temperature 212° F (100° C), or in a dehydrator until completely dry and hard. Store in a sealed glass container in a dry and dark cupboard until needed.

To Make Tea

You need to make a decoction of licorice root, rather than a simple infusion. Place two pinches of dried root and 1½ cups of water in a small saucepan, cover, and simmer for ten to fifteen minutes. Strain the liquid through a sieve or a tea strainer into a teacup. Serve hot. It is a lovely deep orange color with a mild licorice flavor. The sweet, fresh green taste reminds me it is related to the pea, but it also tastes rather like noodles! It has a wonderful calming effect on the body and a slight cooling effect in your mouth. You should reuse the root to make another decoction.

TIPS

Helichrysum petiolare is commonly called the licorice plant, but this plant is not related to *Glycyrrhiza*. Always use the Latin name to be sure you buy the right plant.

Warning: Too much licorice may raise your blood pressure and cause headaches, so as with all the teas, consume in moderation. It is also not recommended for women who are pregnant or breast-feeding.

Tea Bag Friends

- To make a great digestive tonic, blend fennel with licorice. Put a pinch of fennel seeds, a pinch of licorice root, and 1½ cups of water into a saucepan, cover, and simmer on a low heat for 10 to 15 minutes. Strain the liquid through a tea strainer into a teacup. This is a strong and delicious tea. Reuse your licorice and fennel decoction for more than one cup.

- Try blending licorice with ginger for a cold- and flu-defense tea. Make a decoction as before, using a pinch of fresh or dried ginger and a pinch of licorice root. This is a strong tea with a real zing to it.

- Try blending chamomile with licorice for an immune-boosting and cleansing tea. Add a pinch of chamomile to a freshly made licorice root decoction and steep for three minutes. Strain into a teacup to drink.

- Licorice is lovely served with a sprig of fresh anise hyssop to give it a greater aniseed flavor.

Further Plant Advice

The most wonderful thing about growing your own plants is that you can guarantee that no chemicals have been used on them. Make sure all soil fertilizers, plant food, and pest-prevention methods are organic, so as to preserve the ecosystem of your growing space. You should always pick the freshest, youngest leaves of the plant for tea, and use them or dry them on the day they are harvested for the best results.

It is vital that you identify the correct plants, so always refer to the Latin name when buying them. I have listed the plants by their common name and then the Latin name in italic. A system of universal plant classification exists to help unravel a plant's history and help with correct identification. The system lists a plant first by its family (i.e., Apiaceae), then the genus to which it belongs (i.e., *Angelica*). Then a descriptive word or epithet combines with the genus name to make a name for the plant species (i.e., *Angelica archangelica*). Plants can be further categorized into subspecies, cultivars, and hybrids with further subdivisions. It is helpful to know the family a plant belongs to, as this can really help to know the conditions and care the plant needs to thrive.

Many of the plants in this book are perennial and take more than one year to complete their life cycle from seed to making seeds and then dying. An annual completes its life cycle in a year. Herbaceous plants are non-woody plants that die back into the soil to go dormant over the winter and reappear with new shoots in the spring. A shrub is a plant that has woody stems growing from the base of the plant, such as myrtle or rosemary. An evergreen plant will keep its leaves all year round, while a deciduous plant will lose its leaves in the fall and regrow them in the spring.

I have written this book with a temperate climate in mind. Ask your plant supplier for specific growing advice for your own climate and location.

Soil

The key to successful growing is the soil, which should ideally be 80 percent loam and 20 percent humus. Garden soil or loam is a mixture of sand, clay, and silt. Throughout the year you should add organic humus (decomposed plant matter) to your soil. This could be homemade compost from a compost bin, well-rotted farm manure, or mushroom compost. These materials in-

crease soil fertility and improve the texture and drainage of the soil. You can also add sharp sand to help improve drainage if you have heavy soil. When a soil has a good mixture of all these elements it will have a light, crumbly texture. It will be a living soil that will enable your plants and the environment to thrive.

If you have a garden you will need to check the soil pH to see if you have acidic, neutral, or alkaline soil. If the pH is 0 to 6.5, it is acidic; if the pH is 7, it is neutral; and if the pH is 7.7 to 14, it is alkaline. The easiest way to grow plants that do not like your soil type is to make raised beds or use containers that can be filled with suitable soil. If you are growing plants in containers, always buy the best quality organic, peat-free potting soil and add sharp sand, horticultural grit, bark, or perlite to improve drainage, if needed. When growing a plant from seed, you can use a specialist seed-sowing compost, which is sifted to a very fine texture and contains few nutrients.

Mulch is a layer of humus, straw, or other material placed around a plant on top of moist soil to help retain moisture, protect the plant from pests, and provide nutrients for the plant.

Propagation

Creating new plants from seeds, cuttings, or division is one of the most rewarding things to do in the garden. See each plant for specific details.

CUTTINGS

There are three main types of cuttings: stem, leaf, and root. I will focus on stem cuttings (softwood and semi-hardwood), as these are suitable for many of the plants in this book.

Softwood Cuttings

- You use the young new growth of a stem in the springtime to take as a cutting. Plants from which you can take softwood cuttings include geranium, mint, blueberry, lemon verbena, and sage, among others.

- Get a clean pot or container with good drainage holes and fill it with a mixture of two parts of potting soil and one part of perlite (naturally occurring volcanic rock). Perlite helps to improve drainage, which is important as these cuttings can easily rot when exposed to too much moisture.

- Find a non-flowering, young, healthy stem and cut off the top so that the cutting is about 2 to 3 inches (5 to 7 cm) long.

- When you have taken a few cuttings, pop them in a plastic bag and keep them in the shade.

- Cut down the base of the first cutting just below a leaf joint (where a leaf is growing out of the stem), as this is the point from which new roots will most easily grow.

- Remove the lower leaves of the cutting with a knife. Cut off the very top leaves of the cutting to encourage it to bush out.

- Make a hole in the compost using a toothpick.

- If you have access to organic hormone rooting powder, dip the bottom end of the cutting in it to help the roots develop. Most hormone rooting powders contain synthetic plant hormones and so are not suitable for the organic gardener, but you may be able to find an organic variety.

- Insert the cutting into the hole you made in the compost and compact the soil around it to keep secure. Do not push the cutting too far down as you do not want the leaves of the cutting to touch the soil as they can rot if they do.
- Water the cutting from the top by misting it with a sprayer.
- Label your cutting.
- For most softwood cuttings, it is recommended that you place a plastic bag over the pot to help increase the heat and humidity for the cutting to encourage growth. Make sure the bag does not touch the leaves—if it does, use sticks to act as a framework around the plant. Secure the bag to the pot with a rubber band. Remove the bag every few days so that the moisture inside it does not build up too much.
- Place the potted cutting on a light, sunny windowsill and mist it with water most days.
- After a few weeks, the roots should have formed and you can remove the bag. Leave the cut-

ting in the same location to allow it time to adjust to this new temperature. If the weather outside is warm enough (does not fluctuate too much from warm to cold) you can slowly start to get it used to being outside. Place the cutting outside during the day when temperatures are warmer, for longer and longer periods. Bring it in at nighttime initially, leaving it outside the whole time after a few weeks. This process is called hardening off.

Semi-Hardwood Cuttings

Semi-hardwood or semi-ripe cuttings are taken in the late summer or fall, from plants such as myrtle, mountain pepper, rosemary, and manuka. Use the same method as softwood cuttings but add 50 percent perlite or sharp sand to the potting soil as these cuttings need very well-drained soil. It can help to remove the bark from one side of the base of the cutting. Water semi-hardwood cuttings less often than softwood, perhaps once a week, as the weather will not be so warm at this time of year. Keep the cutting inside in a place that gets plenty of light, until it can be put outside the following spring. They can take a long time to root well.

You can propagate *Camellia sinensis* by a type of cutting know as leaf bud cuttings (see Camellia, page 8).

(see Camellia, page 8).

SOWING

Seeds are a great way of getting a lot of plants cheaply. Some plants, however, are very difficult and slow to grow from seed. Seeds need water and moisture to germinate. Using a heated propagator to give warmth to the roots makes seed germination much easier. Some seeds can be sown straight outside. This has the advantage that you do not have to transplant the seedlings, but the disadvantage that you have to wait for the weather to warm up before you can sow. You should prepare your garden by weeding it well, then add some organic humus, which you can mix in as you dig and turn over the soil, and then rake the surface flat. All seeds need the soil to be a certain temperature before they will germi-

nate. Read the specific seed packets for each plant to decide when and where to grow. As a general rule, the seed should be planted twice as deep as the length of the seed, so the bigger the seed, the greater the depth.

A General Guide to Seed Sowing

- Use a good quality seed-sowing compost or seed-starting mix, preferably one that is peat free.
- Fill the seed tray, module, or pot with soil (you can use recycled containers as long as they have drainage holes in the bottom). Drop the soil in gently so it does not compact. Level off the soil by moving your hand across the container from side to side.
- Tap the container three times against a flat surface so that the soil settles below the top edge. You can lightly flatten your soil with a block to create a very even surface, but be careful not to compact the soil.
- Pick off any little stones or soil lumps that may have come to the surface.
- Cup your left hand and tip some seeds into it so that you can use your right hand to sprinkle the seeds over the soil.

- Sow the seeds as thinly as instructed on the seed packet.
- By hand, or using a sieve if you have very small seeds, carefully cover the seeds with a layer of soil or vermiculite.
- Water carefully using a water sprayer or a watering can with a rose, starting the water flowing away from the seed tray. You don't want to wash the seeds away.
- Place the container somewhere warm and light, such as in a greenhouse or on a sunny windowsill.
- Label your seeds with the name and the date as some seeds can take weeks to germinate.
- You can cover your seeds with a lid or plastic bag tied with an elastic band to help increase the humidity around the seeds and keep the temperature relatively constant.
- Water lightly most days with room-temperature water; avoid using cold water. Seeds need to be kept moist at all times but will easily rot if exposed to too much moisture. They will not survive drying out, either, so keep an eye on the soil. Fill up your sprayer or watering can at the end of each watering so that it has come to room temperature by the time you water your seedlings the following day.

TRANSPLANTING

It is crucial to transplant your seedlings before they become leggy and weak, otherwise they will never have enough energy to grow into strong bushy plants. When your seedlings have grown four leaves and you can see their roots appearing through the bottom of the module tray, it is time to transplant them to give their roots more room to grow.

- Fill your pot(s) with organic potting soil/compost and level off the top with your hand.
- Tap the pot twice on a flat surface so that the soil settles.
- Make a hole in the soil according to the size of your seedling's root; if in doubt, make it bigger than you think to prevent the roots from being squashed.
- Carefully lift the seedling out of its pot by squeezing the pot with one hand and lifting the seedling by its leaf with the other. Some seedlings don't like their stems being touched, so avoid lifting by the stem. You may need to divide your seedlings at this point if they have been sown too thickly.

Gently pull the seedlings apart and plant them singly or in small groups of two or three. Mint, coriander, and bergamot can be planted in small groups.

- Lower the seedling into the hole and compact the soil around it, adding more soil if necessary.
- Label your plant.
- Water the plant carefully and place it somewhere warm and sheltered until it becomes more established. When the roots have filled the pots you can repot them into the garden or another container.

DIVIDING

When a perennial plant has either completely outgrown its pot or an older perennial needs rejuvenating, it may be possible to divide it to make into more plants. It is generally best to divide plants in the early spring. Plants suitable for dividing include chamomile, violets, bergamot, and lemon balm.

- Take your plant out of the pot or dig up the plant, making sure the roots are as intact as possible.
- Split the plant using a trowel, a spade, or your hands, dividing it into smaller but still good-sized plants.

- Pot the plants into containers to suit their sizes, using potting compost.
- Compact the soil around the plant and water well.

Repotting

If you are growing in containers you will need to repot your plants every year or so to give the plants more space to keep growing. Spring is the best time of year to repot your plants.

- Choose a container that is the next size up and always make sure it has good drainage holes.
- Put a broken bit of pot, known as a crock, in the bottom of the pot to help further improve drainage.
- Put a small amount of soil into the bottom of the pot.
- Gently tease the roots of your plant to encourage them to grow outward.
- Place your plant into the new container and fill around it with potting soil, pressing down with your fingers around the plant's roots. Fill the container to just below the top of the pot edge with soil.
- Water well.

- Your plant may benefit from a little pruning to tidy it up at this point (you may be able to use some of the clippings for tea). This will encourage new leaf growth and give the roots more of a chance to grow.
- You can also give them a feed with a liquid fertilizer such as seaweed to further encourage growth.

Fertilizers

If your soil is well maintained with humus you should not need to add much fertilizer. It is more necessary if you grow your plants in containers, as there is a limited amount of soil from which the plant can obtain nutrients.

Fertilizers are either organic or nonorganic. Organic means the fertilizer is made from plant or animal matter and nonorganic means it is made from manmade chemicals or mined minerals. Nonorganic fertilizers are highly concentrated and get big results but have a huge impact on the environment. Organic fertilizers need the organisms in the soil to help release the nutrients so they are slower to affect the plant, but they are working in harmony with the environment. Examples of organic fertilizers, sometimes labeled "natural organic fertilizers," in-

clude bonemeal, fish blood and bone, chicken pellets, nettle tea, comfrey juice, worm tea from a wormery, and seaweed. Dried seaweed granules or liquid seaweed is a great choice for a general-purpose organic fertilizer. Seaweed also helps the plants fight pests and diseases. Calcified seaweed is made from calcified and coralline algae so check to see if it is from a renewable source before you buy. Nettles are high in nitrogen (for good leaf growth) and comfrey is high in potash (for flower and fruit growth) and these feeds can be made easily and cheaply at home. Buy a small comfrey plant or divide an existing plant and grow it in a container to prevent its roots from spreading. Nettles are bound to be freely available as they grow everywhere. In the summer the nettles and comfrey will be ready to harvest. Fill a bucketful of nettles or comfrey with water, cover, and leave it for two or three weeks. Make sure you put a lid on, as they really smell. Water down the resulting liquid to 1 part fertilizer to 10 parts water and then use it to water around the base of your plants.

Hardiness

The hardiness of your plants will depend on your specific climate, so this information should be used as a guideline only. In

this book I have classified plants as "hardy," "semi-hardy," or "tender." Hardy means that they are suitable to be grown outside all year round and can withstand temperatures below 5°F (-15°C). Semi-hardy plants may be able to withstand a minimum temperature of between 23 and 5°F (-5 and -15°C) in the winter. During this time, semi-hardy plants should have some extra protection or to be sure, brought into an unheated sheltered environment such as a cold greenhouse or conservatory. Plants outside in containers are more vulnerable as a frost can more easily affect the roots of the plant. Move the plant to a more sheltered position, wrap bubble wrap around the pot leaving the top open so the plant can still be watered, and place a horticultural fleece (available at all good garden centers) over the top and sides of the plants to help insulate them. Horticultural fleece

allows light, air, and moisture to permeate but creates a warmer microclimate beneath it to protect your plants from frosts. Folding the fleece to make more layers provides the plants with even greater frost protection. Remove the fleece during the day if the temperature allows so that the plants will get more light. Other fabrics will not allow enough light to get to your plants and will also absorb water and become heavy, so they should not be used.

If your plant is tender it should only be put outside in warm weather when there is no danger of a sudden drop in temperature. Tender plants will not withstand a temperature of less than 32°F (0°C). Treat them as a houseplant if your climate is not warm enough and try to keep them in a sunny and light place.

All plants, especially when they are seedlings, do not like to have a sudden change in temperature, so it is necessary to harden plants off. This simply means to acclimatize your plant to being outside. If they are used to being inside a heated house they will not survive suddenly being outside (unless the temperature is similar to the inside temperature). It is really useful to have an unheated greenhouse to act as a step to hardening off. Then you can place plants outside for longer and longer lengths of time during the day, and finally leave them outside overnight.

Pests and Diseases

To tackle pests such as whitefly and green-fly, you can make your own garlic spray simply and cheaply. Crush two or three cloves of garlic in a mortar and pestle. Transfer them to a large bowl and add a quart (1 liter) of boiling water. Set aside overnight. The next morning, strain the liquid through a sieve into a bowl, discarding the garlic cloves. Transfer the liquid to a spray bottle. When using garlic spray, make sure you lift the leaves up to spray the undersides as this is where the insects like to hide. Spray the leaves on consecutive days for best results. You can also buy organic insecticidal soap spray for a large infestation if the garlic spray does not work. Nematodes are another biological method of controlling pests like vine weevil, which can be a problem if you are growing in containers. Mildew is a white fungal mold that can be a common problem for some plants such as sage and bergamot. Prevent mildew by not allowing your plants to dry out and making sure they have good air circulation. If you do get mildew, remove the affected leaves as soon as possible and discard them—do not compost them. Spray the remaining plant leaves with milk on consecutive days to help keep mildew at bay. Snails and slugs are always eating my

plants so I try to encourage birds to come and visit. Do not use slug pellets as these are poisoning the animals who then feed on the slugs who eat them. I have discovered that lifting the pots and leaves of large plants to find snails and slugs is one of the best ways to keep on top of them. You can also set a beer trap by burying a glass of beer in the soil, up to the rim for them to fall into. When plants are in the ground you can also try either laying sharp egg shells or putting plastic rings cut out of old drink bottles around your small plants, a pretty effective method if you put them out early enough. I have also found that sprinkling seaweed granules over the soil—as a fertilizer—also helps deter the slugs. The best lesson is to keep on top of any disease or pest and to deal with it early to prevent it taking hold.

Further Tea Advice

Drying Your Plants for Tea

There are various methods of drying plants for tea. You can dry them in an oven, a dehydrator, an airing cupboard, the sun, or simply in the air. The speed and method of drying a plant will affect its flavor. It is not actually the heat but good air circulation that creates the best drying conditions. Experiment with different methods for different plants—what may be perfect for one plant may not suit another. Your climate will also help determine the best method of drying. Any plants with specific drying advice will be listed in its plant chapter. Once dried, tea is best stored in a sealed glass container and kept in a dry and dark cupboard until needed.

OVEN

When using an oven you need a low temperature of 212°F (100°C) or lower for most plants. Use a fan-assisted oven if you have one, to give good air circulation. An Aga has a plate-warming oven, which is ideal for drying plants.

I find the oven good for larger fruits that contain a lot of moisture such as lemons or raspberries, for denser leaves such as myrtle and mountain pepper, and for all roots such as licorice and ginger. Place the plant on a baking sheet or in a baking dish and spread it out in a single layer as thinly as possible. It is important to keep mixing and turning your plant to ensure it dries evenly, so check it every five or ten minutes, depending on what you are drying. Fruits, leaves, and flowers should be dry and crispy to the touch and roots should be hard when completely dry. The oven is the most efficient method of drying flower heads such as roses and calendula. Spread out the heads on a baking

sheet or in a baking dish, allowing lots of space between the flowers. Turn the flower heads every ten minutes and remove when dry and crispy. They may take around forty minutes, depending on the size of flower. When you squeeze the flower it should not be flexible. If it is not dried completely the flowers will go moldy in the storage jar. *Camellia sinensis* leaves need different drying temperatures depending on the type of tea you are making. See pages 10, 14, and 18 for details.

DEHYDRATOR

A dehydrator is an effective drying method, as it creates a constant low heat and allows you to turn the plant throughout the process. The color and texture of the plants stay good, too, so if you are making a lot of tea I recommend buying a dehydrator. They do take a long time—some plants can be in there for twenty-four hours or more—so they can use lots of electricity. Utilize the dehydrator fully each time by drying lots of plants in one go. Fruits and most fleshy/moist plants should go on the lower shelves, as the temperature will be higher. For small roots and plants such as thyme, you will need to line your dehydrator with greaseproof paper or something similar otherwise it falls through the shelves. The dehydrator manufacturer should sell a suitable liner.

RADIATOR OR AIRING CUPBOARD

Airing cupboards provide an ideal environment in which to dry plants. They have a constant warm, dry, and dark environment. However, not many people have airing cupboards anymore, so using a low-temperature radiator when drying plants in the winter is a good alternative. I dry a lot of plants simply by spreading them thinly over a fine-mesh screen and setting them on top of a low radiator. This heat source can be too direct, so place a towel or cloth over the radiator and then set the screen on top. If it is still too warm and the plants are drying too rapidly, you can place the plants near the radiator.

SUN

You can place the screen or baking sheet of plants out in the sun if you have a still (windless) and sunny day. Move the plants around a lot so they are exposed to the air. This method may work well if you live in a hot dry climate but unfortunately, the sun can bleach the color out of the plant and be too harsh.

AIR

Fennel, coriander, lavender, and anise hyssop can be hung upside down to air dry. Hang plants in small bunches so they can dry most efficiently. Tie the stems using a rubber band tight enough that it will remain secure once the plants have dried and shrunk. For delicate seed heads, tie a paper bag over the head to help collect the seeds. In order for this process to work well, they should be hung somewhere dry, warm, and

dark with good ventilation. Take down the bunches as soon as the plants are dry and crispy. When drying plants in the summer you can simply spread out the plants on a mesh or tray and place them in a well-ventilated room, out of direct sunlight, so that lots of fresh air passes over the plants. You need to check them often, moving them around every few hours or so. This can be a gentle method of drying plants such as jasmine or violet flowers and thinner, more delicate leaves such as mint, lemon verbena, or lemon balm and they tend to keep good color when dried this way.

lemon verbena leaves before adding water. Serve with ice and fresh lemon slices and lemon verbena leaves.

To make sweet strawberry or raspberry sun tea, put the fresh fruit and leaves into a mason jar or a jug and proceed as directed above. After the tea has been in the sun for five hours or so, strain the liquid through a jelly bag or fine-mesh sieve into a jug, and place the tea in the refrigerator until chilled. Serve with ice cubes that have fruit frozen inside. You can freeze edible flowers such as violets, lavender, and calendula petals in ice cubes to add as well.

Sun Tea

You can make tea without a kettle using the warmth and energy from the sun. Fruits such as lemons, strawberries, and raspberries are well suited to making sun tea. Place your chosen tea in a mason jar or a jug with a lid, altering the quantity of plant as needed to suit the size of your jar or jug. Add cold water, cover, and place the jar or jug in the hot sun to warm for about five hours. Stir the tea after a few hours. You can serve the tea warm or refrigerate it for two to three hours and serve chilled.

I make a fresh lemon and lemon verbena sun tea by cutting up one lemon and putting it in a mason jar with a handful of

Quick Plant Reference Chart

Common Name	Latin Name	Preferred Position	Maximum Height*	Hardiness†	Level of Difficulty	Can Be Grown Inside as a House-plant
		Sun (S) Part shade (PS) Shade (SHD) Inside (I)* *unless you live in a tropical climate	In feet and inches *grown inside	Hardy (H) Semi Hardy (SH) Tender (T) Annual (A)	Easy (E) Medium (M) Difficult (D)	all year long
Angelica	*Angelica archangelica*	PS	7'	H	E	
Anise Hyssop	*Agastache foeniculum*	S	2'–3'	SH	E	
Bergamot	*Monarda didyma*	PS	3'	H	E	
Blueberry	*Vaccinium corymbosum*	S/PS	4'	H	M	
Calendula	*Calendula officinalis*	S	17"	A	E	
Cardamom	*Elettaria cardamomum*	I	1.5 feet *	T	D	*
Chamomile	*Chamaemelum nobile* *Matricaria recutita*	S S	3.5"–2'	H	E	
Chicory	*Composite Cichorium intybus*	S	3' x 1'	H	E	
Cilantro/ Coriander	*Coriandrum sativum*	PS	24"	A	E	*

Common Name	Latin Name	Preferred Position Sun (S) Part shade (PS) Shade (SHD) Inside (I)* *unless you live in a tropical climate	Maximum Height* In feet and inches *grown inside	Hardiness† Hardy (H) Semi Hardy (SH) Tender (T) Annual (A)	Level of Difficulty Easy (E) Medium (M) Difficult (D)	Can Be Grown Inside as a House-plant all year long
Echinacea	*Echinacea purpurea*	S	30"	H	E	
Fennel	*Foeniculum vulgare*	S	4'	H	E	
Fenugreek	*Trigonella foenum-graecum*	S	15"–18"	A	E	
Ginger	*Zingiber officinale*	I	3'*	T	D	*
Honeysuckle	*Lonicera*	S/PS	20'	H	E	
Hyssop	*Hyssopus officinalis*	S	2'	H (blue variety only)	E	
Jasmine	*Jasminum sambac* "Maid of Orleans" & *Jasminum officinale*	I S	2'* 30'	T T	D E	* *
Lavender	*Lavandula angustifolia*	S	2.5'	H	E	
Lemon	*Citrus x limon*	I	6'*	T	D	
Lemon Balm	*Melissa officinalis*	S/PS	2'	H	E	
Lemon Grass	*Cymbopogon citratus*	S	2'	T	E	*
Lemon Verbena	*Aloysia triphylla*	S	9'	T	M	*
Licorice	*Glycyrrhiza glabra*	S	6'	H (once established)	M	*
Manuka	*Leptospermum scoparium*	S	16'–26'	SH	M	
Mint	*Mentha*	S	2.5'	H	E	*
Mountain Pepper	*Drimys lanceolata*	S/PS	15'	SH	E	
Myrtle	*Myrtus communis*	S	16'	SH	E	
New Jersey Tea	*Ceanothus americanus*	S/PS	3'	H	E	
Raspberry	*Rubus idaeus*	S/PS	6'	H	E	
Rose	*Rosa*	S	depends on variety	H	E	
Rose Hip	*Rosa rugosa*	S/PS	4.5'	H	E	
Rosemary	*Rosmarinus officinalis* "Miss Jessopp's Upright"	S	3'	H	E	
Saffron	*Crocus sativus*	S	8"–12"	H	D	

Sage: Tangerine & Pineapple	*Salvia elegens* "Tangerine Sage," *Salvia elegens* "Scarlet Pineapple"	S	3'–4'	SH	M	*
Scented Pelargonium / Scented Geranium	*Pelargonium*	S/SP	3'	T	E	*
Stevia	*Stevia rebaudiana*	S	2'	T	E	*
Strawberry	*Fragaria*	S	10"	SH	E	
Sweet Tea Vine	*Gynostemma pentaphyllum*	S/PS	19'	H (once established)	E	*
Tea	*Camellia sinensis*	S/PS		SH	M	*
Thyme	*Thymus*	S	12"	H (check each variety)	M	
Tulsi / Holy Basil	*Ocimum tenuiflorum (sanctum)*	S	3'	T	M	*
Violet	*Viola odorata*	PS/SH	3"	H	E	

*Note: the maximum height is the height a plant can grow to given the perfect conditions outside. You can restrict the height of a plant if you keep it in a container or prune it regularly. If the plant is recommended as a houseplant, the height given will be the maximum height it can reach growing in these conditions.

†Hardy: the plant can withstand temperatures below 5°F (-15°C) (USDA Zone 7 and below).
Semi-Hardy: the plant can withstand a minimum temperature somewhere between 23 and 5°F (-5 and -15°C) (USDA Zone 8–9).
Tender: the plant can withstand a minimum temperature of 32°F (0°C). (USDA Zone 10 and above).

Index of Plants

Recommended Sources

Plant and Seed Suppliers

UNITED STATES
Top Tropicals
Jasminum sambac and
Camellia sinensis
toptropicals.com
(866) 897-7957

Camellia Forest Nursery
Camellia sinensis
www.camforest.com
(919) 968-0504

Mountain Gardens
Sweet tea vine (*Gynostemma
pentaphyllum*)
mountaingardensherbs.com
(828) 675-5664

Grow Organic
Seeds, fertilizers, and garden
supplies
www.groworganic.com
(888) 784-1722

Horizon Herbs
www.horizonherbs.com
(541) 846-6233

Burpee
www.burpee.com
(800) 888-1447

R. H. Shumway's
www.rhshumway.com
(800) 342-9461

Richters
Seeds and starter plants
www.richters.com
(905) 640-6677

U.K. AND EUROPE
Plants 4 Presents
Camellia sinensis
plants4presents.co.uk
+44 0845 226 8026

British Saffron
www.britishsaffron.co.uk
+44 01978 761558

Bee Happy Plants
www.beehappyplants.co.uk
+44 01460 221929

Herbal Haven
www.herbalhaven.com
+44 01799 540695

Cockers Roses
www.roses.uk.com
+44 01224 313261

Pennard Plants
www.pennardplants.com
+44 01 749 860039

Groves Nursery
www.grovesnurseries.co.uk
+44 01308 422654

Garden Supplies

Coast of Maine
Organic composts, mulches,
and fertilizers
www.coastofmaine.com
(800) 345-9315

Grow Organic
Seeds, fertilizers, and garden
supplies
www.groworganic.com
(888) 784-1722

Bod Ayre Products
Organic seaweed fertilizers
www.seaweedproducts.co.uk
+44 01806 577 328

Wiggly Wigglers
Composting and wormery
suppliers
www.wigglywigglers.co.uk
+44 01981 500391

Garden Organic
www.gardenorganic.org.uk
+44 024 7630 3517

Empty Tea Bag Suppliers

Burgon & Ball
www.burgonandball.com/shop
(search for "tea bags")
+44 0114 233 8262

Natural Tea Bags
www.naturalteabags.com
(305) 898-5313

Tea Experiences/ Places to Visit

Glenburn Tea Estate &
Boutique Hotel
Darjeeling, India
www.glenburnteaestate.com
+91 98 300 70213

Tregothnan
Cornwall, England
tregothnan.co.uk
+ 44 01872 520000

Charleston Tea Plantation
Charleston, South Carolina
charlestonteaplantation.com
(843) 559-3791

Eden Project
Cornwall, England
www.edenproject.com
+ 44 01726 811911

Recommended Reading

Gascoyne, Kevin, Marchand,
François, and Desharnais,
Jasmin. *Tea: History, Terroirs,
Varieties*. Richmond Hill, On-
tario: Firefly Books, 2011.

Kabuzo, Okakura. *The Book
of Tea*. Eastford, CT: Martino
Fine Books, 2012.

McVicar, Jekka. *Jekka's Complete Herb Book*. London: Kyle
Cathie, 2009.

Moxham, Roy. *A Brief History
of Tea*. Philadelphia: Running
Press, 2009.

Acknowledgments

I am fortunate to have met some wonderful, generous people while researching this book, and I would like to thank them for their help: Emily from Plants 4 Presents, Lorraine from Herbal Haven, Sarah from Bee Happy Plants, Leanne from Cocker Roses, Joe Hollis from Mountain Gardens, and Caroline Riden and Clive Groves from British Saffron. I would also like to thank Burgon & Ball for their support. My very special thanks go to Husna Tara Prakash and Sanjay Sharma from Glenburn Tea Estate in Darjeeling, India, for all of their expert advice on tea processing and growing.

I would like to give a special thank-you to Daniela Rapp, Ivy McFadden, Bethany Reis, Lauren Jablonski, and Eric C. Meyer at St. Martin's Press and to my agent, Isabel Atherton from Creative Authors. I would like to thank Levin Haegele, Rose Finn Kelcey, Frank Williams, Keris Salmon, Mischa Haller, George and Thomas Liversidge, Tom and Jo Howard, Becky and Charlie Willis, Jill Feuerstein, Jane Pearl, and all my friends for their support while I was writing this book. Finally, thank you to Peter, for sampling so many cups of tea and for giving me the confidence to write!